HOW TO

SET-UP AND RUN

A SUCCESSFUL

HOLIDAY RENTAL

(Anywhere !)

DAVID BRENNER

For P...

Contents

INTRODUCTION

Hello – and welcome to the only guide you'll ever need in taking the potentially life-changing step of setting-up and running a holiday rental business. Anywhere you want.

Anywhere ?

Yes – and I'll explain how in a moment, but let me start by telling you a little about myself, and why I've written this book.

My name's David Brenner, I'm a former BBC broadcast journalist and in October 2007, along with my wife Pauline, relocated from Somerset in south-west England to the central Italian region of Abruzzo, where we set-up a holiday rentals business called *Villasfor2*.

To do this, we needed to find a property not only suitable as our own permanent home, but with the added potential of becoming a rentals business too. Then doing whatever building/renovations work was necessary. And finally getting our holiday business up and running.

Which was pretty much what happened between May 2007, when we first saw the Abruzzo property we ended-up buying...

- to November 2007, when we started the purchase process...

- to March 2008, when we completed it...

- then on to the rebuild, which we began in May 2008...

- to when we moved into our house in March 2009...

- and finally to *Villasfor2's* official opening in August 2009

Now, at the time of writing this book, *Villasfor2* is rated by *TripAdvisor* as #1 in Abruzzo in our own particular field of providing villa rental holidays exclusively for couples.

As we've found along the way, while most of our villa rental guests have been holiday-makers, a fair few are also looking to do what we did and buy a property here, with many also wanting to follow in our footsteps and open-up a holiday business.

Naturally enough, they've all been eager to hear about our own experiences; to get any tips we could pass on – and, not least, get an idea of what it all might cost.

But that's not as straightforward as it seems.

Why?

Because thanks to the complexity of Italy's many national and regional property purchase and planning laws – and how these are interpreted and enforced by *comune* (town councils) up and down the country - what *we'd* been able to do in *our* corner of Abruzzo might not have been possible elsewhere in Italy.

Or even in a neighbouring *comune* just down the road.

And in common with every country in the world, property prices throughout Italy vary wildly – as do building and renovation costs, property taxes, legal fees, and the rules and regulations governing rentals.

So as we rapidly discovered, there was no easy, one-size-fits-all formula that could be applied to any property purchase anywhere in Italy. And as a result, no way to come up with a reliable and accurate set of figures I could then pass on to our guests regarding how much *their* proposed plans were going to cost.

Let alone any certainty that a set of building/renovation plans approved in one part of Italy, would automatically be OK in another.

But the more I thought about it, the more I realised that even though the costs of buying and fixing up a property are never the same anywhere in Italy - and that purchase and planning laws can differ from one town to the next - there were certain fundamental principles involved in starting and running a holiday let business that *never* changed.

Even more importantly, it quickly became clear that these principles were exactly the same not only throughout Italy – but wherever you happened to be !

These principles never change or go out-of-date, and they cover *every single aspect* of finding, setting-up, and running a holiday business.

And they apply equally to whatever kind of let you're thinking of starting up – and wherever you're thinking of doing this.

Right from the outset, it's important for me to underline that what I'm *not* going to do in this book is tell you about the legal processes that might apply, or the paperwork you might need, to start your own holiday business project.

Nor what official permits might be necessary; nor what you might have to pay in the way of start-up and/or ongoing fees and taxes to run your business.

Even if that was possible just for Italy - let alone anywhere else in the the world – it'd be impossible to keep that information always 100% accurate and up-to-date.

And if that kind of info's *not* 100% accurate and up-to-date, it's useless – and potentially damaging too. Without even being aware of it, you can end-up breaking local laws, (or sticking to ones that have been changed or dropped), and see your financial plans and budget projections going up in smoke because they're based on old data.

But what I *am* going to do, step by step, is share with you the set-in-stone principles that will govern your project – from the very start, right up to running your business once it's successfully established.

And what gives me the right to pass on this kind of advice ? Because I've done it all myself, starting from scratch – quite literally from bare earth - and ending-up with one of the top holiday rental businesses in Italy.

I'll pass on all the little tips I've picked up running *Villasfor2* – including the one killer question to ask yourself during a key early stage of your own holiday business project that could make the difference between success and failure - and, yes, telling you about the mistakes I've made along the way too, so you can avoid repeating them.

And as a former journalist, I'm going to make all this as easy to read and easy to follow as I can.

Entertaining as well as informative.

Throughout this book, I've worked on the assumption that your plan for running a holiday let will involve moving from the property in which you're currently living, to another. And maybe moving from one country to another too.

Sure, you can start a holiday rental with a 'buy-to-let' property, or may even consider that where you currently live could also be used for a holiday rental business. Perhaps your kids have grown up and left the family home, and you feel there's now some rental potential waiting to be realised ?

To be honest though, unless you live in a recognised holiday destination - where spare space in your existing home might be let via an agency like *Airbnb* (or even offer B&B potential) – it's really only possible if if you already own somewhere big enough to be used both as your own home, and holiday accommodation too.

But if you've decided the moment has arrived in your life for a challenging adventure involving a change of scenery and a new career, in the coming pages you're going to discover exactly how to do this.

Setting-up and running a holiday rental business is a big undertaking that will affect you and your family. It will almost certainly mean a change of lifestyle for you and your partner; have a significant impact on your kids; and might well involve relocating from one country to another.

However, with the right planning and a realistic attitude to what's involved, neither is it all so difficult that you can't go on to become one of the thousands of people worldwide who run a successful holiday rentals business.

So let's start off on that path towards fulfilling the dream...

1. FIRST STEPS

What we'll be covering in the opening section...

- How we got started in our own holiday rentals business

- Is running a holiday business right for you ?

- Key questions about your business you need to ask yourself right now...

- What type of holiday business appeals to you ?

- Your Unique Selling Point

- Who'll be coming to stay ?

- Where do you plan to run your business ? The checklist for your perfect location...

If you're seriously thinking about setting up some kind of holiday business, you might currently be sharing the same nagging doubt that really bothered us when we were laying the groundwork for our own project.

It's the question we get asked more than any other:

"I've got absolutely zero experience of doing this kind of thing. Am I crazy to even think about it ? "

And the answer is – No !

How We Started...

Consider this: I'd worked all my life as a journalist. Pauline's background was in IT Training. Not exactly the perfect background for a new career in the hospitality industry. Especially as our plans were based on nothing much more than our own holiday accommodation experiences.

Basically, while we'd enjoyed staying in good hotels/B&Bs, what we'd liked most were holiday rental/self-catering holidays.

But that was usually a problem.

We don't have kids, so our requirements for a holiday rental were always just for the two of us.

And we found, again and again (and again), that:

- the 'place for two' we'd booked turned out to be slightly smaller than a shoebox.

- or it was great – but part of a big rental complex mostly for large groups of families or friends.

- or the accommodation was just perfect – but as the owners/agents were always quick to point out, it actually slept far more than two, and while there was no problem in renting to just a couple like us, of course we'd have be charged full price. (Or maybe a bit less if we negotiated hard enough).

And the more this happened, the more puzzled we became that the kind of small, affordable, good quality self-catering holiday location just for couples that we were after, just didn't seem to exist.

Or if it *did*, it was an incredibly well-kept secret !

We wondered whether the demand simply wasn't there. Or whether the people who ran holiday rental businesses had figured out the idea of couples-only rentals simply wasn't cost-effective.

But then again, at everywhere we'd ever stayed, there'd always be other kids-free couples like us booked-in too. Could it be that here was a niche sector of the holiday-making public that was being overlooked ?

So we did a little online research. Every single hotel, B&B and self-catering place of the hundreds we looked at both in the UK and overseas offered accommodation to couples – and to families/groups.

But none provided the kind of accessible, *couples-only* holidays we were looking for.

We'd joke that the only way we'd ever find somewhere like this would be to start it ourselves.

And that's how the idea of *Villasfor2* first took root.

To start with, we weren't really that serious. We both had good, well-paid jobs, and the fun notion we'd had about starting a holiday business seemed a million miles away from reality.

But things have a habit of changing...

Over the course of the next three or four years, our professional lives began to seem less sure and clear-cut, to the point where we started thinking seriously about some kind of career change - something that out of necessity would have to be pretty radical, because the problem was that neither of us had any kind of training to do anything else.

Which was what made us start wondering about that pleasant little day-dream we'd had...

All of a sudden, there seemed to be a whole list of questions that needed answering.

And for the first step on the road to *your* holiday business, you're going to have to deal with those same questions too.

Time to start making some notes...

OK...So <u>Why</u> Do You Want To Run A Holiday Business ?

As I've explained, in our case, the answer to this question seemed a possible solution to an enforced career change, which would enable us to earn an income.

What's *your* reason for wanting to do this ?

And why particularly a *holiday business* in preference to something else ?

Start by thinking everything through as honestly and completely as you can, because when it comes to a project as important as this, the key to success is the degree of planning you put in before you start.

Working things out properly beforehand - rather than reacting to what happens as you go along – will immeasurably increase your chance of success, and your chance of bringing things in on time, and on budget.

If something doesn't seem to work, don't gloss it over and think, "It'll be alright on the night."

It never is.

Thoroughly discuss every aspect of your project with those who'll be involved with you. Setting-up and running a holiday business is a big undertaking, which will affect you and your family; will almost certainly mean a change of career for you; and might well involve relocating from one country to another. Do as much research as you can and number-crunch your budgets.

And if after doing all this your plans still seem workable, that'll be a pretty good starting point.

How Are You Going To Do This ? And What's It Going To Cost ?

The nuts-and-bolts logistics of your project.

- How are you going to finance it ?

- What will you live on before you're actually up-and-running ?

- What will your budget be ?

- And what sort of contingency sum do you plan to set aside to deal with unexpected glitches that *will* occur along the way ?

While I can't tell you what your project's going to cost – I *can* tell you what you'll need to allow for to get everything up and running. Or at least what *we* needed...

- The initial property search. Perhaps two or three visits – maybe more - to wherever you've chosen to relocate, to find and buy a suitable property.

- Assorted legal fees, commissions, property taxes and other incidental costs associated with the purchase, and ensuring your planned business is in line with all relevant national and local laws.

- Any necessary renovation and/or rebuilding work, which will include painting and decorating.

- All necessary fixtures/fittings/furnishings and kitting-out for your rental areas.

- If you choose to have one, installing a swimming pool.

- If you choose to have one, planning and planting a garden. And/or landscaping any other areas of your property that need changing.

- Relocation costs from your current country of residence to your new one.

- A contingency sum – usually advised as 10% of your rebuild/renovation budget - to cover 'the unexpected'.

- If you choose to have one, the design, registration, and putting-together of a website for your business.

- A monthly amount to cover all aspects of living in your new country, up to the point where your business is up, running, and generating income.

To achieve this, you'll need a sum of money generated by:

- the sale of your current home

- and/or any capital you may already have

- and/or any income you and/or a family member might receive from a pension or investments

- and/or from any work you're still able to undertake after moving.

Be as honest and realistic as you can with your figures, because it won't actually help in the long-run if you over-estimate the amount of money you're likely to have to pay for everything - but under-estimate what it's all going to cost.

Once you've done your calculations, don't be discouraged - or think it's the end of your plans - if the cost for everything your plans involve adds up to more than what seems to be available

At the very least, you've now got ballpark idea of what you're going to need, and providing there's not a wild discrepancy between income and outgoings, you can adjust your figures to a degree to help level things out.

It's reassuring that you can actually save quite a bit in a variety of ways. For example, we saved a lot of money by sourcing bathroom fittings, doors, windows, tiles - and more - ourselves, rather than leaving this to our builders.

We saved money too by doing much of the decorating ourselves – but *not* any of the construction work. In Italy at least, all electrical and plumbing has to be done by a qualified fitter. Even if we'd had UK qualifications to do this, they wouldn't have counted in Italy, and any work we'd done wouldn't have been officially approved.

Just as important as saving money is ensuring you don't overspend on what you *have* budgeted for. If you've ever watched one of those home makeover, or relocation programmes on TV, you'll know that costs soar when you change your mind about something half-way through a project.

Moving a door, or a window during your renovation/rebuild will ratchet-up the costs, as will spending more than you maybe need to on fixtures and fittings.

In the early stages, getting your rentals built, decorated and finished to a high standard is actually more important than what you do to where you'll be living yourself. Your rentals must look great from Day 1; you can always finish-off or upgrade work in your own home a little later down the line.

It *is* of course a big advantage if your available capital is enough – or say within 10% of what's needed - to cover your likely outgoings, but if you can't get things to balance-out, you have two other avenues open to you to raise the funds you need.

The first is by taking on a business partner. Someone who is prepared to invest money in your project in return for an agreed percentage.

As part of the deal, you – as the business owner/majority shareholder – may agree to your business partner staying cost-free in your property for a certain number of days each year. Perhaps at fixed times too. Your business partner may want a regular return on their investment by taking a fixed sum - or a percentage - of your annual rental income. You in turn may ask for contributions towards annual running costs.

And if and when you finally decide to sell your rental property, you will have to repay your partner's original investment, plus perhaps a further fixed sum or percentage. You may have even agreed to give your partner first option – and maybe even at a pre-agreed price - on whether to buy your property/business.

Clearly, before entering into any such arrangement, the terms and conditions will need to be hammered out in the finest detail and be legally-binding on both parties.

This may seem unnecessary if your business partner is a family member or close friend, but it's actually of benefit to everyone to know exactly where they stand right from the start, and that their respective interests are clearly set-out and fully protected.

Another finance option is to consider taking out a mortgage or other similar loan.

Your ability to do this will vary from country-to-country, and it might be hard to set up somewhere you've just moved and consequently have no financial standing or credit rating and – at least at the time you make your application – no job.

But if you prepare a convincing enough business plan – and if you *do* have some regular income from investment or other employment coming in - some lenders will be prepared to advance you something based on your business's projected income – with the value of your property and any land as collateral.

What Type Of Holiday Business Would You Like To Run ?

When it comes to the kind of small-scale holiday business you can run yourself, you basically have a choice between a holiday let – or a B&B. But though both have the same end-product in providing holiday accommodation, the setting-up and day-to-day running of these businesses are very different.

We considered both options, but pretty quickly opted for holiday lets - and the reason we did this was because it seemed to us that running this type of business was a lot less demanding than running a B&B.

What's best for you ? Running a Rental ? Or a B&B ?
At the very start of of our own planning, we had an open mind as to which of these routes we'd take.

We opted – as you know - for holiday rentals, and the reason we did this was because although there are regular 'must-do' tasks common to both rentals and B&Bs, it seemed to us that a rental allowed for a much more flexible schedule for taking care of these tasks than a B&B.

But the real clincher was that a B&B's daily schedule is built-around breakfast. Which in turn means an early start and hitting the ground running for the property's owners throughout the holiday season.

On every single day of the year when you have guests staying with you – and during summer, that hopefully should be for several unbroken weeks at a stretch – breakfast has to be available at a fixed time each morning.

No ifs, buts, or "terribly sorry breakfast is late - we overslept".

And if guests have an early flight home and want breakfast before they leave, you can't really say no, can you ?

(Well...you *can*...but then don't expect to see 5-star reviews on *TripAdvisor* praising you for putting yourself out and going the extra mile...)

You'll also need to think carefully about what you're actually going to offer to your guests for breakfast each day. Or, more to the point, what your guests feel they have a right to expect – like a traditional, cooked 'Full English', rather than a simple 'continental' rolls and coffee.

(And it's funny how those who make do with a cup of tea and a piece of toast when they're at home, really like to go to town when someone else is doing the cooking and the washing-up !)

I know that some B&B owners take real pride in rising to this challenge of laying on a lavish and delicious spread every morning, even including freshly-baked breads and home-made preserves, and genuinely don't mind the extra demands this makes on their time.

But regardless of whether or not you pull out all the breakfast stops each day, as a matter of course if you decide to go down the B&B route, you'll also need to make provision for any guests with special dietary requirements; to decide whether – if you accept family bookings – you provide any 'Kids Options'; the actual food preparation, serving, and cleaning up afterwards; and – not least – what the costs of the food and preparation are likely to be, so you can factor these in to your charges.

That's not quite all either, because guests will generally expect their beds to be made each morning, with their bathrooms also wiped-down and towels hung up. And public rooms used by all B&B guests – usually at least a breakfast room and a lounge/TV room – will need to be kept clean and tidy.

It *is* a demanding and uncompromising schedule – and means every day is heavily front-loaded. But B&B owners I've spoken to say the general aim is to get the daily chores finished by lunchtime, which – theoretically at least – allows them to regard the afternoon as 'down-time'.

In contrast, in the workload we've evolved in running *Villasfor2*, there's just one regular task that needs doing every day throughout the holiday season.

Around 8.15 every morning from early May to late September, I clean the pool. This involves no preparation and nothing more arduous than removing any leaves/bugs that might have dropped in the water since the previous morning. And while I'm at poolside, I'll also straighten-out the sunbeds, and if needs-be, give the pool sun-terrace a quick sweep.

The whole process takes about 15 minutes; ensures the pool's looking at its clean and sparkling best if a guest fancies an early swim; and also gives me the chance to look over the grounds and gardens to make sure everything is as it should be.

Aside from cleaning a pool, there are of course plenty of other regular tasks we need to take on – as will you, if you choose to run a holiday let. I'll be telling you about all these in much more detail in the coming pages, but for now, it's enough to know that unlike a B&B's daily to-do list, these tasks don't have to be performed at the same time each day.

Or even *every* day.

That considerable degree of flexibility I've mentioned really does allow you to set your own schedule – and that in turn lets you manage your work-time - and your down-time - much more effectively.

Why work harder when it's so much easier to just work smarter ?

Who Will Be Working With You ?

Running *any* kind of holiday business isn't something you can do on your own. You'll need at least one additional person working alongside you. That of course can be your partner, or if your family is joining you in this new venture, some of them might be willing and able to help out too.

Additionally, depending on the scope of your business and the amount of land you might have, you could think about hiring regular or part-time staff – or think about paying for help on an as-needed basis.

Let me explain how Pauline and I divide-up the responsibilities of running *Villasfor2*. Essentially, Pauline looks after everything going on *inside* our rental villas. I take care of everything *outside*.

If we had job titles, Pauline would be 'Head of Housekeeping' – and I'd be 'Estate Manager' !

Pauline's responsibilities are getting each of our three rental villas cleaned and readied after one set of guests check-out and before new arrivals check-in. And with three villas, that can often mean 'multi-changeover' days, with the corresponding doubling – or even tripling – of her regular workload. There's the laundering of all towels and bed-linen – and changing these as necessary during a guest's stay; ensuring the furnishings and fittings are all in good order, and all standard villa supplies are topped-up; and taking care of any necessary maintenance, repairs and redecoration.

Plus looking after our own house too.

In its own way, our plot of one acre (approximately 4000sqm) is just as important an aspect of our business as our rental villas. Not much point in having outstanding holiday accommodation if it's set on an untended, weed-infested plot, along with an uninviting, murky swimming pool. So my responsibilities centre-around ensuring that the pool and our land are always well looked-after.

As I've mentioned, the pool gets a daily clean during the early May – late September period when it's open, plus other bits/pieces of semi-regular maintenance. Our land is divided into an orchard, vegetable plot, flower-beds, grassed areas – and a few olive trees. All need different routine care to keep them looking good. I also manage the business side of *Villasfor2,* which involves keeping tabs on our website and social media presence; looking after enquiries and bookings; and keeping the books.

And we sort-of share the daily dealings with our guests !

Since opening our business in 2009, we've evolved a work schedule that works smoothly and efficiently for us, balancing periods of intense activity with the downtime that's essential to recharge our batteries.

And of course our work is seasonal, with the vast majority of our bookings between May and September. The off-season allows us time to take care of larger maintenance jobs we don't get the chance to do in summer – and there'll usually be a trickle of guests too. Generally – but by no means always – December and January are the only months when we can be classed as 'empty'.

For one person, the schedule would be an impossibility. For two – as we've found – it's perfectly achievable. Even if – like us – you've had no previous experience at all in this line of work.

There's no denying however that some of the tasks we undertake are physically demanding, and if this makes you uneasy, the best bit of encouragement I can give you is that we were both in our late fifties – and neither of us especially fit or active - when we left the UK, moved to Italy, and set-up *Villasfor2* – which we've since run well into our late sixties.

At the beginning, we found the workload associated with our new business unfamiliar and demanding, both mentally and physically. And yes, more than once, we wondered just what we'd let ourselves in for.

But as with any job, with each day comes growing experience and familiarity, and the assorted tasks that initially had seemed so difficult and time-consuming gradually started getting easier.

In the very early days, we regularly paid for outside help for big physical tasks that were just beyond our resources and capabilities – like the landscaping of our acre plot. Since then, with more experience, we've developed our own way of dealing ourselves with pretty much everything that needs doing.

Just about the only exception to that is looking after our olive trees, which needs the kind of specialist equipment – and expertise – that we just don't have. Spread out over the year, this doesn't cost a huge amount – and it's justified by the annual end-product of a few litres of our very own organic, extra-virgin oil each autumn. Some for us – and some for our guests !

Now, there's no reason at all why you can't decide to try and make your life easier and less demanding, by paying other people to take on some of the jobs or responsibilities, you feel you can't - or would rather not - do yourself.

But there *is* one very good reason why this isn't a good habit to adopt. It's because whatever you pay other people comes out of your business income, and therefore means less for you.

Of course there'll be the occasional task that's simply too big for you to realistically accomplish on your own – like looking after our olives. And specialist jobs involving a plumber or an electrician have to be paid for too. But paying someone else to do work that you could do yourself becomes a difficult habit to break if it becomes the norm rather than the exception.

In the process of getting to know your new business and how it all works, almost automatically you'll evolve a way of working effectively and efficiently. It happened to us – and it'll happen to you too. It'll very much be *your* way of doing things. Not necessarily better. Or by working harder or longer. Just...different.

Who's Coming To Stay ? And Why ? (Discovering Your USP...)

When we first moved to Abruzzo in late 2007, there were something like 70-80 available holiday rental properties throughout the entire region.

At the time of writing this book in 2017, *TripAdvisor* alone lists nearly 1200.

That's a rise of around 1500% in ten years – and it's still growing.

This just emphasises that at any large or small holiday destination anywhere in the world, there's going to be a degree of competition for business among accommodation providers.

And as you're going to be an accommodation provider yourself, you'll need a compelling reason why a holidaymaker should want to stay with you, rather than your competitor down the road.

In marketing terms, that 'compelling reason' is known as the Unique Selling Point – or USP . It's the major factor that sets you apart from the competition, and persuades potential customers to choose your product, rather than someone else's.

If, right from the outset, you have a clear idea of what the USP behind your holiday rental is going to be, it's going to greatly simplify not only identifying your future guests, but also setting-up your business in the right property, and in the right location.

At its most basic, if you're thinking of attracting 20-somethings and capitalising on a vibrant city nightlife scene in a cool urban location, you're not going to buy a countryside property; neither will you be offering opportunities to go mountain biking or rock climbing from a beachside base; or singles holidays in a property set-up for family groups.

You get the idea...

So then...

- where do you see your market ?

- And what will be *your* USP ?

Or to put it another way,

- who's going to pay to stay with you ?

- And why should they want to stay with *you*, rather than the place down the road ?

Before we started *Villasfor2*, I had only the very vaguest idea of what was actually meant by 'marketing', but it did seem basic common sense to:

- Decide who we'd aim our villa rentals at.

- Discover if any other accommodation provider was already going after our chosen guest target.

- And if that turned out to be the case, to come up with a plan for offering those in our guest target a better - or *different* - service or product to what was already available elsewhere.

So start by thinking about *your* possible market.

You may want your your potential guests to be people who may not be especially well looked-after in a particular aspect of the existing rentals market. Or if they are, then you want them to be looking for something different/more attractive/more exclusive – or just simply *better* - in some key aspect than anything else around.

If there's a gap in the existing holiday rentals market for what you're going to offer – you want to fill it.

Once you've got an idea of your target market, start thinking about holiday destinations where your plans might work well – and just how you intend putting those plans into practice, and setting yourselves apart from anything in the same line that might already be on offer.

And while you're thinking about your rental market and unique selling points, there'll be another important factor for you to consider...

Kids vs No Kids...and Groups vs Couples
We took the decision very early in our own setting-up process that we would *not* cater for either kids...or family/friends groups - and at some point early in your own project, you're going to have to deal with this question too.

Why will you need to decide early ? Because in planning and setting-up sleeping arrangements and general accommodation in your rentals, you'll need to know whether or not to make provision for kids. That's not something you can leave to the last minute, as it'll have an important bearing on the type of property you decide to buy.

It's a kind of chicken-and-egg situation....

- Do you go ahead and buy a property – and then decide on your likeliest market based on its layout and room configuration ?

- Or do you start off with a clear idea of the holiday market you want to target - and then search for the property best-suited to your ideas ?

After we'd first decided our own unique selling point was that we were going to offer holiday rental accommodation exclusively for couples, it made our eventual property search a lot easier. So when we began that search, we were looking for a place that provided the best fit for what we wanted to do.

Similarly, if you decide to welcome both kids and groups, you'll need to bear this in mind when you begin looking, so that what you end up buying readily lends itself to accommodating these types of guest.

In fact, a rentals set-up capable of accommodating – say – a group of adult friends, or a family group, is actually pretty similar nowadays.

As regards British guests in particular, the traditional 'nuclear family' of Mum, Dad and a couple of kids isn't really the norm any more, and in terms of a 'family group', you're more likely to get Mum and Dad; two sets of kids from previous marriages; Mum's sister and *her* kids; and a couple of grandparents !

And that – in terms of the actual number of people who'll be staying with you – won't be much different to a group of 10-15 adults.

Provided your property has the space to comfortably accommodate everyone, you won't have a problem.

However...

If you *are* going to accept bookings for kids, you'll need to consider some important practicalities:

- You'll need to decide whether or not to establish a separate price structure for kids in your rental charges.

- If you have a pool, it'll have to be kids-safe.

- The same will apply to access in and around your property - and stairways.

- You'll need to add bunk-beds – or similar; and/or cots – to your shopping list when fitting-out your rentals...

- ...plus the necessary bed linen, mattresses and mattress protectors. (Because accidents happen...)

- If you accept families with babies, think about nappy-changing facilities – and nappy disposal too...

- ...plus secure, dry storage for baby buggies.

- And while most parents will cram their luggage with things to keep the kids amused if it rains, as many DVDs and games that *you* can muster won't go amiss either.

- Finally – washing machines and dryers. I'll deal with these in more detail later on, but kids do seem to get through an awful lot of clothes on holiday...

As we found out when researching out own set-up, the overwhelming percentage of rental owners welcome bookings from family groups; *and* adult groups; *and* couples.

But this can make for an uneasy mix, as it's generally the couple that comes off worse in this kind of situation.

Why ? Because - as we've been told by our own guests many times - if you go away on your own, without kids, you don't especially want to then share your holiday with other people's.

Additionally, if a couple find themselves sharing a rental's facilities with a big group, guess who's going to feel marginalised ?

Finding a really effective USP is an elusive task. We've all experienced the free toiletries and the welcome packs of food and wine; and I've come across rentals making a big point of providing top luxury-quality towels and bed-linen; or a free meal in a good local restaurant.

They're all absolutely fine. A really nice bonus for their guests.

But as regards choosing where to go on holiday, would any of them *really* provide the clinching argument ?

As I explained earlier, we started thinking about a holiday rentals business offering accommodation just for couples, on the basis that nowhere else seemed to be doing this.

Then we went a little further. Not only would we offer rental holidays just for couples, but we'd also specifically exclude kids and larger group and family bookings too. This allowed us to *guarantee* to our guests that they'd be spending their holiday in a kids-free zone, *and* only with a few other couples, rather than a large group.

That's something we found that in our chosen destination, no other rental could match, and as we've discovered it's a USP that works, and is a genuine plus-point for us.

Other alternatives ? Well – you can of course do completely the opposite to what we did and make a point of emphasising that you *do* specifically welcome groups and/or kids. Aside from rentals like ours that specialise in accommodation for a specific type of guest, we've come across highly successful holiday rentals that additionally offer..

- long weekends for stag and hen parties

- food and wine-based activities. Cookery classes; artisan food production; general food and wine tours; and – especially – winery visits

- arts-based activities, including photography, painting, and ceramics, as well as museums and galleries.

- historical tours. Our local area has several good Roman sites. City-based rentals usually have easier access than rural rentals to museums, galleries and notable buildings.

- adventure and activity holidays, from mountain-biking and riding or trekking to hiking, canoeing, rock-climbing or rafting.

- if you have a small rental, that can genuinely be described as 'romantic' and 'tucked away'; and with particularly good facilities, think perhaps about exploring its specific potential as a honeymoon destination.

- if you're lucky enough to have a particularly impressive, spacious and generally high-end rental, set in an equally splendid location, you could even – if local laws allow – market yourself as a wedding venue !

For these – and any other attractions that your chosen area, (or your rental itself), suggests – you need to make yourself an expert in guiding your guests towards activities and opportunities they wouldn't otherwise have found for themselves.

And in looking to attract guests likely to be interested in the specialist activities available in your area, you'd also need to know about the specific websites, social media pages, societies or publications where you can pitch your message to reach them.

Where Would You Like To Go ?

The options here are pretty straightforward and clearcut:

1. Staying in your existing property.

2. Relocating to somewhere in the same country where you're living now.

3. Relocating to a different country.

Option 1
We've already established that unless you already live in a holiday destination within your current country of residence, and can readily convert your existing property into a self-contained home for you, and at least one other self-contained rental unit, it isn't really an advisable or realistic suggestion.

Option 2
Staying in whichever country you currently live has several significant advantages. And possibly several equally significant disadvantages !

The Advantages:

- You won't need to learn a new language.

- You'll retain the familiarity of how your current country *works*. Banks, shops, currency, TV programmes, the health system, newspapers, food – and so much else – will stay the same.

- It'll be much easier to keep in close touch with your friends and family.

- If your kids are involved in the move, they won't need to get to grips with a new school system.

- Removal costs will be far lower than they would be if you

moved to another country.

- If things don't go according to plan, it'll be easier to pick up the pieces in a familiar country.

- If most of your guests will be coming from within your own country, they won't have to bother with arranging payment in a different currency – and you'll be largely immune from exchange rate fluctuations.

The Disadvantages:

- If your current country of residence – and the area in which you intend running your holiday rental – isn't a recognised and popular holiday destination with a working tourism infrastructure.

- If your country/proposed rental area is not served by a good international air network, or is otherwise difficult for visitors to reach.

- If the main holiday season – be it summer or winter – is short.

- If the weather is unpredictable during the main holiday season.

- If language/communication with local people is likely to be a problem for visitors.

And don't forget either that if you *do* change countries, all the advantages listed above for staying where you are now, in terms of not having to learn a new language, and being on safe and familiar territory etc, become possible deal-breaking *disadvantages*...

As far as our own project was concerned, once we'd decided to pursue the idea of running a holiday let aimed at couples, our first choice – for precisely the reasons I've outlined above - was to do this somewhere in the UK.

Which resulted in a very sharp reality check.

The UK's a small country and the popular holiday areas are well-known, clearly defined, and – as we quickly discovered - extremely well-served with a massive choice of holiday accommodation.

Add to that, the UK property market when we actually began our search in 2004 was sky-high. Even more so in popular, much-visited holiday areas. To buy the kind of property that would've given us a place to live *and* rental accommodation was completely beyond our financial reach.

So we checked out existing holiday rental businesses for sale in a few areas of the UK that appealed to us. That turned our to be even more of a non-starter, because in addition to home + rental accommodation, the fact that an existing business was also part of the deal sent prices spiralling even higher !

Add to all that the sheer amount holiday rental accommodation available in the UK, and it quickly became clear that even targeting a niche market like couples, we'd be setting ourselves a very stiff challenge.

Perhaps, for a couple of complete beginners in the holiday business, an unrealistic challenge too.

Attempting something new in an already saturated market didn't seem an especially sensible starting point - which moved our search on to...

Option 3.
The question that now needs answering is if you're going to leave your existing comfort zone; move to another country; and start-up a holiday business – where's that going to be ?

For us, coming from the UK, our search area was going to be somewhere in Europe. We did briefly consider the New England area of the USA, but in reality for us, this was a logistical non-starter, as were other established – but long distance - holiday destinations like the Caribbean and south-east Asia.

Realistically, our decision to remain in Europe was a no-brainer for vital-to-us reasons of accessibility, practicality, and familiarity. Where *you* decide *you'd* like to be will be governed by the factors that are important to you – and of course wherever in the world you happen to be living right now.

As far as we were concerned, once we'd decide that staying somewhere in Europe offered the best potential outcome for us, narrowing-down the search to just one country wasn't that difficult.

Use our check-list below as the basis for noting your own key factors, and narrowing-down where you'd like to be.

Our own part-professional/part-personal 10-Point Checklist – in order of importance – looked like this:

1. Our chosen country should be a popular European holiday destination...

2. ...with a good food and wine culture.

3. Ideally, it'd be a country where we'd been on holiday ourselves...perhaps more than once...so there'd be a degree of familiarity. Perhaps even some language skills. And it would have to be a country where we'd actively like to live permanently.

4. It would have to be reasonably quick and straightforward to permanently relocate to our chosen destination and start our planned business.

5. There would need to be good availability and access to a wide range of local amenities, from shops, restaurants, petrol stations and supermarkets to doctors, dentists, local schools if you have kids – and if you have pets, a vet !

6. We'd want to be in a region of that country not already saturated by mass-market tourism. Somewhere a little off the beaten tourist track...

7. ...but nevertheless not so remote and undiscovered that it had

no facilities for visitors, and we'd be the area's first holiday-providers. It was important too that in winter, we'd still be able to get around easily.

8. Wherever we chose for our holiday business, there'd need to be good accessibility by air and road (and maybe even by rail too). And flights to our chosen destination would have to operate year-round; be reasonably frequent (say 3-4 times a week); with at least one flight each weekend.

9. To maximise income from our rentals, our chosen destination should have a long summer holiday season; be worth considering too in spring and autumn– and the possibility of nearby winter sports facilities would be a real bonus.

10. There should be a good range of available and affordable housing with holiday rental potential.

And the winner was...

...Italy !

And more specifically...

...Abruzzo !

Why ? Let's revisit that check-list...

1. Our chosen country should be a popular European holiday destination...
   Every country in Western Europe markets itself as a great for holidays – and Eastern Europe's steadily opening-up by offering itself as 'undiscovered' and providing terrific value for money. To start with then, we were faced with a huge choice of possible countries. With so much available, it seemed a good starting point to our search...

2. ...with a good food and wine culture.
   Why was this so such a big consideration for us ? Don't forget we were moving somewhere not just to start a business – but to live

permanently too. So while location and surroundings were very important, so too was the basic infrastructure of everyday life. We enjoy good food and wine, so its easy availability was a big factor for us. And of course, good wines and good places to eat out are plus-points for any holiday destination too.

A list that initially contained pretty well every country in Europe was suddenly narrowed-down to a highly personal choice of three probables: France, Italy and Spain. And three possibles: Portugal, Germany and Greece.

3. Ideally, it'd be a country where we'd been on holiday ourselves...perhaps more than once...so there'd be a degree of familiarity. Perhaps even some language skills. And it would have to be a country where we'd actively like to live permanently.
    That set of considerations effectively eliminated Portugal, Germany and Greece from the running, as none of the three were places we could see ourselves living long-term. The sheer unfamiliarity of the Greek language and alphabet was another major drawback too.

    France and Italy remained very much in contention. Both were countries we really liked and had visited frequently. Between us, we spoke reasonably good everyday French - and a little not-very-good tourist Italian !

    Spain was a problem. We both appreciated its huge popularity as a holiday destination, but neither of us knew the country well enough to pinpoint a particular region as good for us to live and work. And our knowledge of how to speak Spanish was virtually non-existent. So Spain ended-up not making the cut...

4. It would have to be reasonably quick and straightforward to permanently relocate to our chosen destination and start our planned business.
    Once we'd decided where we wanted to live, we wanted to press ahead and get things moving as soon and as quickly as possible.

As far as we could, we wanted to avoid getting caught-up in a web of bureaucracy which would delay – or even prevent – our plans. To achieve this, specialist legal knowledge for our chosen area was absolutely essential – and we needed to discover as a priority if this would be available wherever we decided to settle.

5. There would need to be good availability and access to a wide range of local amenities, from shops, restaurants, petrol stations and supermarkets to doctors, dentists, local schools if you have kids – and if you have pets, a vet !
    No matter how good a location seems, it's going to lose its charm for both you and your guests very quickly if key local amenities aren't within easy reach. And if you need a doctor/dentist/vet – which sooner or later will *be an absolute certainty - you need to be reasonably confident of being able to get this kind of appropriate professional help quickly and easily when you need to – and to ensure that any medication you take regularly in your existing country will be available in your new country too.*

    Europe as a whole is good for state-run health systems, but you need to find out if – and/or when – you'd be allowed to use it. And how you'd cope in any interim gap between this point and your arrival.

6. We'd want to be in a region of that country not already saturated by mass-market tourism. Somewhere a little off the beaten tourist track...
    With our choice of destination now between resting between France or Italy, we needed to think about where *in those two countries would be a good place for us to move.*

    France's tourism-magnet hotspots seemed so numerous and well-known: Normandy; Brittany; the Loire valley; the Dordogne; Provence; the Riviera; and of course Paris. Was there anywhere left where people would actually want *to go on holiday ? Where was 'undiscovered' France ?*

    Italy seemed very similar. Mass-tourism emphasis here centred on the the quartet of Rome, Venice, Naples and Florence. Plus Tuscany, the Italian Riviera, and the famed Tyrrhenian coastline south of Naples.

On a holiday in Tuscany at a very tentative stage of our relocation search, we looked at property for sale in local papers and estate agents' windows. We loved the region – still do – but realised right away that our likely budget would be completely unrealistic in enabling us to buy the right kind of property to live and run a rentals business.

(A realisation that in fact was no bad thing, as sometimes it's just as important – and time-saving - to know the areas that are way beyond your budget, as it is to know the ones that aren't...)

But Umbria, Le Marche, Abruzzo and Puglia seemed to have definite 'undiscovered' potential. As did Sardinia and Sicily.

7. ...but nevertheless not so remote and undiscovered that it had no facilities for visitors – and we'd be the area's first holiday-providers. It was important too that in winter, we'd still be able to get around easily.

    In drawing-up lists of possible destinations in both Italy and France, it seemed too much of a risk setting ourselves up as holiday rental pioneers in completely 'undiscovered' spots. We wondered whether it's actually possible for a place to be too remote, and whether the reason it's 'undiscovered' is because it's difficult to reach and doesn't have much to offer once you've arrived !

    So during our subsequent property search, if somewhere did seem a little too far off the beaten track, it always made us ask ourselves if we'd be OK spending a week or two there on holiday ourselves without going stir-crazy.

    And while it's not always easy, if you can, visit places you like the look of in winter. Pretty well everywhere is at its best and most appealing in summer, but...

- *if you still like the look of it on a cold, gloomy winter's day*

- *if all the places open for visitors in summer are still open for locals in winter*

- *if the roads are kept clear when the weather's bad, and it's reasonably easy to get around for your day-to-day needs*

- *and if you could definitely see yourself happily living in the area when there's perhaps not much to keep you occupied...*

You could be onto a winner !

8. Wherever we chose for our holiday business, there'd need to be good accessibility by air and road (and maybe even by rail too). And flights to our chosen destination would have to operate year-round; be reasonably frequent (say 3-4 times a week); with at least one flight each weekend.
France's close proximity and accessibility to the UK; the Channel Tunnel and ferries; the superb French autoroute and TGV rail systems; and numerous regional airports with regular connecting flights to most of Europe – and the rest of the world too – gave the country a major boost in our ratings.

   Not that Italy was badly-served. In general, the autostrada and high-speed rail networks are both very good, as is the spread of regional and international airports. What made us uneasy about Italy though was that while the transport links were especially good in the north of the country, they started becoming less good the further south you got.

   And looking a little further south in Italy seemed attractive to us...

   As regards accessibility, most guests will fly from their home country to your nearest airport, and won't want a lengthy drive after their flight. A good rule of thumb to remember during your upcoming property search isn't so much the actual distance between the airport and your property – but the time it takes to get there.

We reckon anything up to an hour or so is ideal. Anything longer can be OK if the drive's easy. But think very carefully if the drive is likely to be difficult – especially on unfamiliar roads, in an unfamiliar rental car - and/or at night after a late flight arrival.

9. Our chosen destination should have a long summer holiday season – and the possibility of nearby winter sports facilities would be a real bonus.
    In our own experience, summers in Italy – or at least summers in <u>holiday</u> Italy - just seemed to start earlier and go on later; be less prone to bad weather; and be simply hotter than in France.

    (I'd stress the 'our experience' angle. It was a highly subjective, unscientific and unskilled point of view !)

    What was a bit of a surprise however was the scope of winter sports resorts in Italy. We'd always assumed these to be only in the Alps and Dolomites, not realising that the Apennine chain stretching down Italy's backbone is big winter sports territory too.

    I have no idea whether in terms of ski resorts; or the total number of lifts; or any other similar statistic, France or Italy is the 'bigger' winter sports country. What does seem the case though is that Italy offers more accessible facilities over a wider part of the country than does France.

10. There should be a good range of available and affordable housing with holiday rental potential. *This condition decided us on where we should at least start looking for a suitable property. Certain areas of France unquestionably offered great value – but those areas weren't especially our top relocation choices. Initially, the parts of Italy that appealed to us just seemed to offer an ideal combination of affordable, available property in interesting and accessible holiday locations.*

Narrowing down the search...
So having decided to begin our search in Italy – and having already

38

written-off Tuscany - we started by looking at Tuscany's neighbour, Umbria.

At this stage, we weren't at all concerned about beginning to look for specific properties, as the most important initial factor was just seeing as much of the region as we could during a week-long first visit; getting a feel of its general property market; and just touring round and getting to know the area a bit to see whether or not we'd actually like to live there.

In the event, Umbria didn't measure-up for us – and neither did its coastal neighbour Le Marche. The reasons were purely personal and subjective and simply came down to whether we felt comfortable and confident about the possibility of permanently relocating to either, and running a business there.

As it happened – we didn't.

Next on the list was Abruzzo, one stop down the Adriatic coast from Le Marche. It wasn't love at first sight – but for the same personal, subjective reasons which had made us reject Umbria and Le Marche, we certainly found it intriguing.

To a greater or lesser degree, Abruzzo seemed to fulfil all the criteria on our wish-list. To be more specific, the area of southern Abruzzo between the sea and the Majella National Park.

Abruzzo in fact has three spectacular National Parks - wonderful protected landscapes of mountains and forests, which was one of the factors that initially attracted us to the region.

We liked the contrast between confident modern towns and quiet rural villages that didn't seem to have changed much in decades; an excellent food and wine culture – with astonishingly low prices; and we were excited by equally low prices in the housing market too.

As regards running a holiday business – while Abruzzo's Adriatic coastline is a magnet for Italians in August, it's uncrowded during the rest of summer – while there were, (and still are), large areas inland that were, (and still are), unspoiled by mass tourism - but still well-enough visited by holidaymakers who value its amenities, leisurely pace of life and overall value for money.

And while the coast had hotels and other accommodation alternatives aplenty, we were encouraged to find a small, established - but developing - number of inland accommodation providers. Even more so that these mostly seemed to be owner-run rentals and B&Bs.

If the region hadn't had any – or just a scant few - accommodation providers, it would've set alarm bells ringing. But it just seemed a good sign that other owners already had sufficient confidence in those inland areas to set-up businesses there.

The key to Abruzzo for us was that the parts we especially liked were rural – but not remote. The region has its own international airport - plus good road and rail links to the rest of Italy, and beyond into Europe – and perhaps best of all, at its closest point, it's just an hour outside Rome's eastern edge.

Hold on just a minute !
You talk about being 'encouraged 'to find a number of existing holiday accommodation providers already operating in southern Abruzzo – but how did you discover this information ? In fact – how would you discover this information about anywhere else !

It's not that difficult.

The easiest and quickest way is to go onto one of the big, global holiday rental sites like *TripAdvisor* or *HomeAway* and see what they have on offer in the region. And then to check-out what the rental providers you come across are offering in terms of accommodation – and to whom.

In our case, we particularly wanted to find out not only the size of the existing rentals market n southern Abruzzo, but also if anyone was targeting accommodation just for couples.

What we turned up on our research was enough to prompt us to take things a stage further by exploring the region a little more thoroughly – and seeing if we could find somewhere just right for our own business...

2. FINDING THE RIGHT PROPERTY

In this section, I'll be telling you about -

- The Killer Question to ask yourself at the very start of your property hunt

- The right type of property for your business

- The pros and cons of installing a swimming pool

- Location. Location. Location. Choosing the perfect spot

- Starting your search online

- Buying privately – or through an agent

- What to look for in a good agent

Having worked through the general basics surrounding running a successful holiday rental, it's now time to start talking specifically about how to find exactly the right property in exactly the right location for your new business venture.

I've just outlined the process we followed that helped us identify the Italian region of Abruzzo as a potential destination for our project. Our next step was deciding what type of property we actually needed for our 'couples-only' rentals – and taking a look at the region's property market to see if it was readily available.

Going online is an incredibly valuable way of getting an initial feel of what's on offer in any given area, and what it's all likely to cost. But there's a limit to what even the best property website can tell you.

At some point, you're going to have to take a trip to the area that's attracting you, and see for yourself what it's actually *like* – and what your money will buy.

To do that, you'll need to have a pretty good idea about what you want.

And to help you decide, you first need to know all about...

The Killer Question

I can tell you now that the property search you're about to undertake will be different to any other you've ever done.

Because with any property you've ever bought before, the most important question you've probably had to ask yourself is, "Would I like to live here ?"

And you're still going to be asking yourself that question - along with another that's *much* more important.

So much so in fact, that if you get the answer wrong, it could quite literally decide whether your rentals business is a success – or a failure.

That killer question, which you should be the first thing you ask yourself during your upcoming search, *about every single property, the minute you set eyes on it,* is:

"Would I like to come here for my holiday ?"

Take a minute to think about this....

Until now, you've looked at any property you might have been thinking of buying; weighed-up a list of pros and cons; and asked yourself whether it'd be right for you and your family.

Those considerations will still be important – but now, they'll be secondary to a much more important set of criteria, because now, you have to look at property not just as somewhere that ticks all the boxes as your new home - but through the eyes of your incoming guests...

Imagine yourself as someone who's booked a holiday with you. They've chosen to stay with you because when they were looking online, or through some agency, they wanted to come to your region; they liked the look of what you had to offer; plus the excellent reviews you've hopefully received; and the fair price they'd be paying for a holiday with you.

43

But of course, even though they might have seen – and been influenced by – great photographs of your property and its surroundings, they've never actually seen it all *for real*.

And as you'll know yourself from *your* experiences of booking a holiday somewhere you've never been before, that no matter how many great pictures; or rave reviews; or mouthwatering descriptions you've seen, you weren't finally convinced you'd made a great choice *until you'd actually arrived.*

So just like you were, your new guests will be a little apprehensive about what they're going to find.

And, again from your own experience in this kind of situation, you'll know the rush of relief and excitement you felt when you arrived; got out of the car; grabbed that first all-important glimpse of where you'd be staying; its setting; and its surroundings, and went, "WOW !"

It's the best-possible start to a holiday – and it's *exactly* the same great feeling you want all your guests to experience when they arrive at your place.

Not a lukewarm, "Er...this is...nice..."

It won't be the best of starts if your guests start their holiday feeling disappointed and let-down.

As that old saying goes, 'You never get a second chance to make a first impression...'

This is why asking yourself 'The Killer Question' each and every time you take your first look at a potential property on your upcoming search is of such importance. Because if *your* very first glimpse of somewhere you're thinking of setting-up your business makes *you* go "WOW !" it's a pretty good bet that a guests will have a similar reaction.

And the answer to, "Would I like to come here for my holiday ?" will be, "YES PLEASE !"

What's Right For Your Business ?

Time to make some crucial decisions...

Do you want a property in a seaside/rural...or city/town/village setting ?
The simplest answer might be where *you* want to live...and/or what your guests might like to do on their holidays !

Some rental guests love urban settings, with the sheer convenience of having local shops, bars and restaurants all within walking distance of where they're staying – plus nightlife, nearby sights, landmarks and attractions and the general buzz that comes from the lively hustle and bustle of local street-life.

Yes, it'll probably be noisy - (unless you live in a suburb...and a suburb is hardly an ideal holiday destination...) - but then again, you don't book an urban holiday and expect it to be quiet.

Bear in mind though that an urban setting could mean you won't get as much land as you would rurally. (Or even any). In turn, that could impact on whether or not you have room for a pool. (Not a problem if a pool doesn't figure in your plans – but see below !) A town/village location also might present problems for on-street parking. But again, if you have room, a carpark with space for one car per per lettings unit – and your car too - would be a big plus.

A seaside/rural location usually offers more in the way of tranquillity; extra space; and perhaps better views too - but it could also mean that having a car is essential to get around, and the extra cost of this might be a drawback for some guests.

As a rough rule, seaside and rural properties tend to rent-out very well during summer – but less so during late autumn and winter. Town and city properties, particularly those in historical and/or capital city locations, seem to be well-occupied throughout the year, with no particular highs or lows. Additionally, urban properties do seem to offer greater scope for weekend breaks – especially out-of-season.

However you're much more likely to be able to provide a rental suitable for a large group of adults and kids in seaside/rural locations than you are in towns and cities. Additionally – regardless of where you see your rental market lying - you're also more likely to find the potential for self-contained rentals at the seaside and in the country than you would in an urban setting, where you could well find yourself renting-out part of your own home.

As with all else in this exercise, it comes down to a trade-off between where you and your family would ideally like to be based – and the general desirability of this as a holiday destination offering excellent potential to run a rental business.

How much land do you want ?
Speaking from our own experience, *Villasfor2* is set on around 4,000 square meters (about an acre) of south-facing hillside in olive groves and open countryside. We could have bought more adjoining land – and I'm really pleased we didn't.

Why ? Well – in our original plans, we wanted enough land for a pool; and a carpark; and a garden; and a vegetable patch; and an orchard – and maybe a few chickens; perhaps even a goat ! As I mentioned earlier, there were already a dozen or so olive trees on the land we bought, but there were (literally) hundreds more trees on adjoining land, which we could've bought cheaply.

It all seemed a great idea, but it was only when we sat down and seriously thought about what we might have been taking on that reality kicked-in.

We were moving to Abruzzo to run a holiday rentals business – not to run a small-holding, or be olive oil producers.

So while we *do* have both a veggie patch and an orchard, we didn't follow-up the possibility of buying more land/olive trees, nor chickens or a goat. But, as I mentioned earlier, I've now evolved a routine that enables me to look after the land and keep our pool in good shape – but prioritise our business and our guests.

(And give me the necessary down-time as well...)

Of course you may find that you can handle the responsibility of more than the acre of land we have – especially if you've got family members to help out.

Or you may decide you don't need as much.

In a rural setting, your plot size will probably be sufficient to include everything you think you can definitely handle. In an urban setting, the space available will almost certainly mean you have to compromise ruthlessly about what you want – and what your guests will expect.

Somewhere they can spread out and relax under a shady tree, or on a sun terrace; or a pool; or even just somewhere to park the car safely, will be more important than your veggie patch or chicken run.

Whatever plot size you end-up with, it really does need to be generous enough so the amenities you're going to provide don't end-up being squeezed into the available space. Remember too your land is just as important a part of your holiday rental as your actual accommodation, and so has to be kept well maintained and looking good.

As it'll probably be the first thing your new guests will see as they arrive, the state of your land will be part of that vital first impression.

Choosing the right building...
Or to put it another way...

- How do you see where you'll be living in relation to where you'll be renting-out ?

- Do you want one building for you and your family ? And another just for guests ?

- Or will just one large building that can be divided into a home for you, plus rental units, be OK ?

- And how many rental units do you plan to have ?

From the outset, you'll need to decide how many rental units you want. When I'm chatting to people thinking of starting a rental business and ask them this question, I generally get a puzzled look and told, "Well...one..."

And that's absolutely fine - if you plan on catering for large groups. And if that's the case, you'll need a property capable of accommodating up to around 10-15 adults and kids at one time.

(But don't even consider catering primarily for large groups – and then think about using a couple of leftover rooms as a rental for just a couple of people. That would just about work OK if you had just a couple – and nobody else – renting with you. It definitely would *not* work if the couple found themselves sharing everything with a big group of family and friends.)

On the other hand, you might want to go down the route we chose, and deliberately aim to provide accommodation for couples; or perhaps two couples sharing. If you choose this option, then – unless your income expectations/requirements are low - just one rental unit won't be enough.

The bottom line here is that much as you might like it otherwise, if it's to be successful, your rental *cannot* be all things to all people. It's a case of catering *either* for one large group of family/friends sharing what will in practicality be a single rental unit comprising multi-bed/bathrooms, plus kitchen and communal living space; *or* a series of smaller units, each having independent bed/bath room(s), kitchen and living space, and each holding something like 2-6 people.

Incidentally, talking about bathrooms – and of special relevance if you intend having just one unit to let-out to a group – is the ideal ratio of bathrooms to guests. Renting out to just two people at a time, this isn't an issue that's ever concerned us, but it becomes *very* important when you've got a group of 10+ people sharing.

Ideally, for this kind of lettings unit, the usual norm is to allow one bathroom for every four guests.

More or less...

With ten guests, you'd try and fit three bathrooms – plus an extra toilet. If your guest capacity is twelve people or more, at least three bathrooms - plus a couple of extra toilets if your plumbing/budget can cope.

For a unit for 4-6 people, if there's only one bathroom, you'd need an additional toilet. For 8-10 people – two bathrooms.

And however many bathrooms you have, you'll need to ensure your boiler can deal with the demands that are going to be made on it. Far better – and I think preferred by the majority of guests – is to fit showers instead of baths. They're quicker, use less water, place less of a strain on your boiler, and take up less space.

Of course it goes without saying that if you're going with any number of smaller lettings units, each must have its own bathroom.

How many rental units *is* enough ? The answer depends on how much money you need to make. Which in turn will depend on whether your rental is going to be your sole source of income, or to top-up what you'll be receiving from pensions, investments, or capital.

I'll be going into the financial aspects of running a rental in a lot more detail in the next section of this book, (which will also deal with getting your business off the ground), so take a look at that – and then factor-in the bits that are applicable to your plans as you decide the type and size of property that's going to provide the best fit for your plans.

Clearly though, if you plan on accommodating big groups, unless you buy a very, (very) substantial property, it's going to be a problem fitting a large number of adults and kids – and your own family – all under one roof.

Regardless of whether or not that's physically possible, the basic question here is whether you'd actually *want* to share what is basically your home with so many people ? Or more to the point, would your guests want to spend their holidays sharing one large building with *you* ? It's almost certain this arrangement would be unsatisfactory and inhibiting for everyone

Having just one building in use both as your home and your rentals can only really be a successful and viable proposition if it can be readily divided into one part for you; and smaller, self-contained unit(s) for guests.

And by 'self-contained', not only do I mean a completely private area having its own dedicated facilities, but also an area that has its own private guest entrance too.

A possible compromise might be if your property has a front door opening into a lobby from which one door leads to your own accommodation, and another leads to where your guests will stay. Otherwise it really won't work if your guests have to pass through any other part of your home to reach theirs.

When we began our property search in Abruzzo, the idea was to buy an old farmhouse – which would become our own home - and then convert existing outbuildings like sheds and barns into our rentals.

As I'll explain a little later, this simply wasn't legally possible in our Abruzzo search area - and made us rethink our plans. On the other hand though, it quite definitely *is* an option elsewhere in Europe – and perhaps even in other parts of Italy – and most probably elsewhere in the world too.

Knowing for absolute certainty what you can/can't do with a property you're thinking of buying is where you really do need expert, unbiased help. In our experience, the best place to get this is at the planning office of the local town hall.

In our experience, local officials were always delighted to give us their advice, and it really did help establish relationships that served us well further down the line. If they don't speak English – or if you don't speak the local language – perhaps try social media or local expat groups for someone to give you a hand.

Choosing To Buy What's Right For You

You've basically got a couple of choices. Do you want to go for a fixer-upper ? Or somewhere that's basically ready to move into ? Either choice has big plus – and big minus – points.

A Fixer-Upper...

- Will always be cheaper than somewhere that's ready to move into.

- Offers more flexibility in reconfiguring the layout to suit your rental plans.

- Offers scope for enlargement that might not be available with a ready-finished property.

- And you can choose the colour schemes, fixtures, fittings and finishes *exactly* how you want.

But on the other hand...

The big question is just how much 'fixing up' needs doing ?

- The cheaper a property is is, the more that will need doing. And the more that needs doing, the longer it will take. And the longer it takes means the more it will cost to do, and the longer it'll be before your rentals business is up-and-running.

- And while all that repair and renovation's going on, where are you actually going to live ? And what are you going to live on ?

- The problem with buying what's essentially a broken building is that you're actually not going to discover everything that needs doing until the work's started. Nasty surprises tend to stay hidden – like the state of the plumbing and electrics - and tend to be expensive to fix.

- Before you start any remedial work, you'll of course consult with a designer or architect to get plans drawn-up so the finished product will be exactly how you envisage. Then – depending on the amount of work that needs doing – those plans might need to be approved by local authorities. That adds another layer of time and money.

- And, based on those plans, you'll ask at least two builders to give you cost and time estimates of the work involved. Irrespective of who you choose to do the work, if you've ever watched any makeover, rebuild, or renovation programme on TV, you'll know that no build project in history has ever come in exactly on-time and exactly on-budget.

Somewhere ready to move into...

- Lets you start-up your business and start making money with the minimum delay.

- Will possibly allow you to live there from day 1, ruling out the need to find any temporary accommodation.

- Will be structurally sound and in good order. At most, it might need redecorating to your tastes.

- Might also offer scope for enlargement.

- Could be the best option if you intend using the building purely as your own home, with a separate building(s) used for your rental unit(s).

- Will probably need less in the way of fixture and fittings in the kitchen and bathrooms - and heating – (all of which are usually already installed) than a property that needs renovating.

But on the other hand...

- The property will be much more expensive to buy than a fixer-upper.

- There will be little or no flexibility to reconfigure the layout to suit your personal/rental requirements.

- There'll be less opportunity to put your 'stamp' on this type of ready-finished property.

- Even though the property is structurally ready to move into, you might still want to install new bathrooms/kitchens, plus upgrade existing plumbing, boiler capacity, and wiring – which will add to the already higher cost.

Talking of costs incidentally, the most frequently-asked question about a fixer-up project is, "How much will I have to pay ?"

We asked this question ourselves, and the answer we always got was a ballpark €1000 per square meter.

But nobody would – or could – tell us what we would actually *get* for this. Would €1000 per square meter fix up any kind of wreck ? Would it buy us marble floors – or cheap tiles ? Would we get a luxury bathroom and kitchen – or budget versions ? Wood-framed windows – or aluminium ? Underfloor heating – or radiators ? These were issues that always seemed to be fudged.

Let's say your property is 150 square meters. Using the €1000 per square meter formula, you'd need to find a fairly hefty €150,000 to renovate. It sounds a lot. And it probably *is* a lot. Possibly more than you'd need, unless the property needs structural work, in addition to cosmetic repair and renovation,

Much better to just talk to a couple of builders – and any other professionals involved in your project; get a consensus view on what needs doing and what it'll cost; and then decide a realistic, affordable overall budget for your project, split between construction work – and any new fixtures and fitting you'll need.

One tip I can pass on is that on our own project, we saved a considerable sum by sourcing as much as possible ourselves in the way of doors, windows, tiles, kitchens and bathrooms – and much more.

Our (excellent) builders didn't much like us doing this, as it probably cost them the commission they'd have got from using their own regular suppliers – but it helped us keep a lid on costs, and when it comes to spending – or saving - your money, that's a crucial factor.

Are there other options ? Yes there are. Instead of buying a fixer-upper, or a ready-to-move-into property, buy a ruin, demolish it, and rebuild from scratch.

Which is what we did.

Not many people do this, (in fact, we've only come across a tiny handful who have), but it was incredibly quick to do and enabled us to get exactly what we wanted in terms of where to live, and where to rent out.

It's easier to keep a lid on costs with a new-build, and you can incorporate all the safety and energy-saving measures you want, so the property is economic to run and maintain.

I also have to own up and say it's actually quite cool having a house built to your *exact* specifications. You normally think of this as being the exclusive preserve of the rich and famous, when in fact it's nothing of the sort.

I appreciate completely a new-build may not be an option for everyone – and definitely not for you if your heart is set on some kind of 'character property' - but it's really worth considering when nothing you've seen quite works for you.

There is one final option – a variation on the 'two properties' theme – which is to buy one place for you and your family to live...and another reasonably close-by to be your rental.

Not an ideal solution, and not an especially practical one – unless you want to keep your personal family life as separated as possible from your business life, or the property which would be your rental simply doesn't have the space to accommodate you alongside your guests, (or vice versa), and you have no other option but to buy another property elsewhere.

Optional Extras ? Or Essentials ?

Heating and Air-Conditioning

Unless your rental property is going to be located somewhere the temperature reliably never ever drops below 20°C , day or night, 365 days a year – you'll need some form of heating. Wood and pellet burners and open fires are all highly desirable, but they *do* need cleaning out; they *do* need somewhere to stock whatever fuel they burn; and they *do* need someone to keep an eye on them.

Which will usually mean you.

If whatever building work you're doing to your property allows it, install underfloor central heating in preference to radiators. The initial outlay is a little more (but not ruinously so) and it's *much* cheaper to run using either gas or electricity. An underfloor system is also less intrusive than radiators and if properly installed, is then virtually maintenance-free.

If your property already has a central heating system, you need do nothing more than ensure it works !

If you're looking for green heating options, then explore the different types of solar panel available; heat exchange systems – and even wind. We have photo-voltaic panels installed on our own property – they *do* work and they *do* keep our electricity costs down.

But be aware that taking the eco-friendly route is a *highly* specialised area and your builder might not have the necessary technical expertise or experience to give you the right advice and/or installation service.

Air-conditioning is tricky. If your budget runs to it , then yes – it can be a good selling-point for you. And a virtual necessity if summers do get very hot for long periods. On the other hand, every now and then, it can become not much more than an expensive-to-run toy

Air-con isn't particularly expensive to install, but it can be *very* expensive to run – so if it *is* on your list of amenities, you'll need to be OK entrusting the unit's remote control to your guests and then keeping your fingers crossed they won't leave the system running cranked up to the max from the moment they arrive, to the moment they leave.

In our experience, that's happily rare – though not unknown ! Usually, once the air-con's novelty has worn off, guests just turn it on to cool down and stay cool – and turn it off/down when they are.

Yes, air-con can be a bit of an expensive luxury, but we've found it's such a popular feature in our own rental units that it'd always be on our list of 'must haves'.

Pool ? Or no pool ?

If you have the space and the budget, I'd have absolutely no hesitation in recommending you have a pool installed. Yes, it can represent a sizeable investment; yes, it needs a degree of continuous care when it's in use to keep it in perfect condition; and – if your business is going to be located where the pool will only be open during the summer – it might strike you as something of a waste having this major asset that's only used for four or five months each year.

Even so – it's worth it.

Having checked with your local authority/water supplier that it's permissible to install a pool at your property, you then have the option of in-ground; above-ground; or sunken/semi-sunken installations in a wide wide variety of shapes and sizes – which you can have heated or unheated; plus choices of lining materials and colour; and filtration systems.

As we did, I'd always go – within reason - for the biggest pool you can afford, on the basis that this'll buy you a proper *swimming* pool – as opposed to the budget options of splash pools, or even just large kids' pools, that some owners install.

A pool that allows your guests to have a proper swim - as opposed to doing little more than just stand around in water - provides a real focal point for your rental, and if you make room for a sun terrace alongside, complete with sunbeams and umbrellas, (which will take up roughly the same surface area as the pool), you'll have a perfect feature where your guests can spend an entire day.

We know from our reviews just how important a pool is when holiday choices are being made; and though it may possibly allow you to charge just a little more for your rental prices, the most important point is that having a pool instantly puts you one-up over other accommodation providers who don't.

As a guide, our own pool measures 11 x 7m (roughly 36 x 23 feet); and holds 80,000 litres (approximately 20,000 gallons).

Two additional points:

- If kids are going to be using your pool, you may well need to think in terms of a small adjoining pool where very young children can happily splash about; while for safety reasons, your main pool might need to have a uniform – and fairly shallow – depth, as opposed to 'shallow; and 'deep' ends.

- If you opt for an in-ground pool, be aware that that you'll need to dig a very large hole in which to put it - and then think of what to do with the resulting pile of earth. Our 80,000 litre pool displaced a bit more than 80,000 kilos of soil – which translates into around 80 tons. We used this to to provide the foundation of our pool sun terrace and a bordering garden.

Are there reasons for *not* installing a pool ? The two most common are a lack of available space (which of course you can't do very much about) – and the cost involved.

And on that latter point, the costs aren't exclusively about the initial installation.

A pool *does* cost money to run.

- there's the electricity you'll use on the pump that keeps the water circulating, which can be for up to eight hours a day, every day the pool is in use – and at peak electricity charge times too.

- plus a water-heater if you have one.

- there's the water you'll use to keep the pool topped-up, (as you'll be astonished how much can get lost to evaporation during a hot summer).

- and – if your pool is chlorine-sanitised – the chemicals you'll need to buy. (We originally had a salt-water sanitiser fitted, before switching over to an ultra-violet system when that wore out. They're both more expensive to install – but are much more pleasant to use than a chlorine pool, and once in use, much cheaper to run than using chemicals).

Neither is a swimming pool a one-off, set-and-forget addition to your holiday rental. Mechanically, it's pretty simple: a pump to keep the water circulating; and filtration and sanitising units. Usually, these are extremely reliable, but like anything mechanical, no matter how well cared-for, they *can* go wrong and eventually they *will* need replacing. Same goes for pool liners.

Given a decent standard of pool equipment at the time of installation, and subsequent good care, you'll easily get at least a decade – and longer - trouble-free pool enjoyment. Just be aware though this won't be forever.

Of maybe lesser concern - as I've mentioned - a pool also needs a degree of daily attention to keep it clean and in tip-top condition, but from personal experience, I can guarantee this isn't a deal-breaker.

In fact, if your budget runs to it, you can get hold of a pool-cleaning robot which will decrease your daily commitment to the absolute minimum.

Location. Location. Location. (Or why we looked at 96 properties...)

Did we *really* look at 96 properties before finding the one we bought ?

Yes, we really did.

So what were the criteria that made us look at so many ?

Following exactly the same steps I've just outlined, we'd decided we wanted to buy property in a rural location; with some land, (but not too much), which would primarily give us space for a pool.

As I've mentioned, our original plan was to buy something like an old farmhouse for us to live in, and then convert any outbuildings into our holiday rentals. Which seemed like a great plan until we got told that in our favoured part of southern Abruzzo, legally, this wasn't permissible.

Time for a rethink...

We didn't *really* fancy buying just one large building to subdivide into home and rental units, so the search became a case of finding a building for us, and - as converting barns, sheds, or hen-houses was now off-limits – something else alongside with the potential to turn into our rentals.

And – largely because nothing else had really occurred to us – we swayed towards a fixer-upper, rather than somewhere ready to move into.

That was the relatively easy bit...

Then it started getting a bit harder.

96 properties harder...

Why so many ?

Because we had a very specific set of criteria for the property that was to become both our home and our business, of the places we saw, we knew the minute we pulled-up outside 75% of them that the basic setting was just completely wrong.

No getting away from the fact that you can have the most perfect property, but if it's tucked away down a side street; or is in a rundown location; or has rowdy neighbours whose kids play Europop at full blast; or has a wonderful view of the local industrial estate; or is miles from the local shops and amenities; and even further from the nearest airport – you're just not going to have that elusive WOW ! factor.

(To be honest, in most instances we just kept on driving, as there was no real point in stopping to have even the briefest look round.)

Of the remaining 25% we got as far as looking round, the vast majority just didn't offer,

- the right kind of accommodation

- or not enough – or even too much – land

- or were just fine – but impractically far from travel links and local amenities.

A very, *very* few were good enough to make us think hard. In the end, three were good enough to make us want to buy them.

And three times, those prospective purchases fell-through.

No deep or meaningful reasons why things didn't work out – just a combination of Italy and Italians which was – though we didn't quite see it that way at the time – a very useful introduction to the way Italy works and thinks.

Then, in May 2007, just a few days after seeing our third prospective purchase go down the plug, we finally found what was destined to become our home – and *Villasfor2.*

And as it happens, property #97 was so right and so perfect in every respect, we ended-up being vastly relieved that none of our other possible purchases had actually happened.

Which was probably just as well, because it seemed by that time we'd seen just about every property for sale in and around our favoured part of southern Abruzzo, and got to know most of the local agents.

In fact, we 'd seen so many properties, that when we were unknowingly taken back to see one we'd already viewed – I didn't recognise it.

But Pauline did – and told me so. However I was adamant we'd never seen the place before.

The argument was quickly and definitively settled when Pauline showed me a photo of the property we'd taken first time around. (Worryingly though, I *still* didn't really recognise it !)

This little instance underlined the importance of taking at least one photo, even of somewhere you wouldn't have the remotest intention of buying. If nothing else, it'll jog your memory about what you've seen – and what you haven't.

In brief – Our own case history
Why was property #97 so perfect ?

- Because it offered not one, but *two* individual buildings on the same 1-acre plot.

- Both were derelict and had been abandoned some forty years previously.

- One of these ruins was earmarked as our own future home; the other – an old barn – was destined to become our rental villas.

- Fortunately, the barn had been used as a dual-purpose dwelling and cattle shed, so we were able to obtain planning permission for our planned conversion.

The original temptation was to carefully restore both buildings, using the lovely, cream-coloured local stone from which they'd been originally built. However, this would have taken a long time – and a lot of money – and as our absolute over-riding priority was to get our rentals business up-and-running, it was easier, quicker, and certainly cheaper, to knock everything down and start again.

Here's the timetable of our build...

- October 2007 – First payment on the properties, with commitment to buy

- March 2008 – Final payment and sale completed. Between October and March, we'd drawn up building plans with our architect – signing them off on the twelfth set of drawings – and had informally discussed them with our local council to ensure there'd be no major problems getting them approved. We formally submitted our new-build project for consideration the day after the sale was finalised.

- April 2008 - Planning permission approved.

- May 2008 – The old ruins are demolished and the site is cleared. Then it rained for a month...

- June 2008 – Work starts in earnest. We contracted our builders to work on-site every day until the project was complete. This was to avoid the practice (in this part of Italy at least) of builders working a week or so on my project...then going off to do some other work...followed by a month somewhere else...then back to me. With speed of the essence, we needed our building crew on-site all day, every day.

- March 2009 - Work on our house is finished – and we move in. We completed our own house first – rather than the villas – because if we'd done it the other way round and then opened for business, people would have been spending their holiday amidst the noise and work of our house being finished-off. And who wants to spend a holiday on a building site ?

- July 2009 – Building work on the villas is complete, and we take a few weeks to kit them out and ensure everything works as it should. The pool – installed around the turn of the year – is also ready.

- August 2009 – *Villasfor2* officially opens – and we welcome our first guests.

Our build time set local speed records – and there were two reasons for this:

- We didn't so much as change the position of a light-switch from the finalised plans, as to do so takes time, and costs money.

- And because we were living in a rental property just a short distance away throughout the build, we paid a visit to the site every single day to ensure things were kept ticking over.

Handing over large sums of money at regular intervals helped things along too !

Looking Online For The Perfect Property

I'd imagine that pretty well *all* property hunts today start online – and it's not that different regardless of whether you're looking for something where you live at the moment, or in another country.

You're probably familiar with the big international property sites like *Rightmove* and *Prime Location* – and they're as good a place as any to start looking.

However...

Most of the properties you'll find on these sites will be expensive.

That's because it costs a *lot* of money to buy space on these big sites. (Which in turn places them beyond the reach of most private sellers.) The overwhelming percentage of listings are posted by property agencies, who buy a page or two of blank space, which they then fill with a regularly-changing choice of properties currently on their books.

They won't cover what this costs through the commission they earn on the sale of any cheap places they advertise, so while there might be one or two of these to catch your attention, the bulk of those advertised will be high-end.

Maybe not exactly what you're looking for...

But persevere, because aside from the big international agents you'll find with an online search, dig a little deeper and you'll start coming across agents based in your chosen country. Go just a little further still, and you'll finally come across agents based in your chosen search areas – and properties that fit your search parameters.

And although, as with the big international sites, the bulk of the advertised properties you see will be listed with agents – a little more online research, will allow you to start building-up contacts in specific areas that interest you. You'll find available properties in all price ranges - and some will be owned by private sellers too.

Buying From An Agent – Or A Private Seller ?

While you might come across a private seller online, once you've started looking in earnest in your chosen location, you might be surprised how many private sellers start appearing and want to see you !

Word gets around !

The owner; or the desk clerk; or the barman; or the waiter where you're staying on a property hunt will at some point probably ask what brings you to their part of the world. So of course you'll tell them, and more often than not, you'll learn they have a relative; a friend; or a friend of a friend who just happens to have a place for sale nearby.

Or go into a local bar and tell the barkeep you're property-hunting and ask if they know anything in the area. If they don't, someone at the bar invariably will !

This is all good fun, and can genuinely give you a quick feel for a local property market, but unless you and a private seller can comfortably communicate in a shared language, or you can set-up some cast-iron protection of your interests, I would personally be more hesitant about going down this route, rather than dealing with an agent, as there are too many areas in which a deal can go wrong.

The one big plus point about buying from a private seller is that you save any commission fees that you as the buyer...or the seller...or both of you, would be liable to pay if you were buying through an agent. (And who pays what varies from country to country).

By dealing direct with the seller, you're much more likely to negotiate a better price than you'd get dealing with an agent.

But if you *do* decide that a private seller's got the exact property you want, at the very least hire a lawyer, (preferably someone who's been independently recommended), who speaks English as a first language – or if possible, even your own native language if that's different - to protect your interests in the purchase process, and from the outset, establish two key points:

- that your seller in fact legally owns *all* of what they're selling. (i.e. that no third-party has a prior claim to all/part of it).

- that you're actually buying what you *think* you're buying . (i.e. perhaps you're under the impression the deal includes the entire plot of land on which the property stands, instead of - in reality – maybe just half of it).

And of course *never, ever* hand over *any* cash to *anyone* under *any* circumstances without your lawyer being present, and without being given a signed receipt.

Dealing with an agent provides three important elements that a private seller can't match:

- in most countries – though not absolutely everywhere – it's mandatory for a property agent to have an operating licence issued by an official regulating body that oversees businesses practices and codes of conduct. This means – theoretically at least - that should something go wrong with your purchase, you have somewhere to raise any issues.

- while a private seller can offer you only one property for sale, an agent can give you access to many. (Beware of anyone claiming to be a private seller who seems to have a large property portfolio).

- unlike a private seller, an agent sells property in a daily basis, and so is much more likely to be familiar with the easiest, most cost-effective and quickest ways to buy property in their local area.

But as with a private seller, if you're buying through an agent, you should still get yourself a lawyer. It's actually not uncommon in some countries for an agent to provide a 'package' sales service which will involve,

- having a property structurally checked-out

- access to local builders who'll do any repair/restoration work needed

- a lawyer to see-through the purchase

- and perhaps even local financing if you need a mortgage or loan.

That can be a pretty tempting proposition, especially as it'll be offered to you as a great way of saving time and money, rather than going to the effort of buying-in local help yourself.

We used our own lawyer, (and our own architect too, to advise on whether the property we wanted to buy was genuinely suited to our plans). Yes, this cost us extra. (Though in the greater scheme of things, as a percentage of the overall property package cost, not a very great deal extra). But the peace of mind and confidence it gave us were priceless.

How To Find A Good Agent

The first contact you'll probably have with an agent is through a website. Speaking for the part of Italy in which we bought, we're impressed that an ever-increasing number of sites are available not only in Italian – but usually in English, German, French, Spanish, Polish, Swedish, Dutch, Russian and Chinese too !

That's not to say of course that all agents have a team of linguists on stand-by in their office – their sites will simply have been professionally translated – but it *is* evidence of an understanding that property purchase nowadays is international.

Speaking only English rarely presents a problem anymore, but if it's not your first language, with a little advance notice, a good agent will usually find someone to communicate with you.

And if a website is well put-together; works on whatever platform you want of either desktop; laptop; tablet; or smartphone; is easily navigable; has a decent range of the type and price of property you're looking for; and you get a prompt response to a call or email – that's a good start...

A good agent will listen to what your plans involve and then do their best to show you what might be suitable – even if that's just one single property.

But you'll probably come across those who'll waste your time by showing you everything they have on their books, in the hope that one might possibly fit the bill. (Which you'll quickly discover if you've asked to see rural houses – and start getting shown seaside condominiums...)

But be aware of...
Once again passing on our experience buying in Italy, we found that as regards our plans for opening a villa rental, agents – *all* agents - would

67

tell us exactly what they thought we wanted to hear.

Or to be rather more cynical, they'd tell us anything to secure a sale...

Let's go back to what we originally wanted...

Something like an old farm. The main farmhouse would be our own home. We'd convert any outbuildings, barns etc into our rental units.

Every single agent who showed us property assured us this was a great idea and wouldn't present any problems.

Except it wasn't actually true...

Under the rules and regulations that applied in 2007 - and as interpreted by local councils within our search area - while you could do pretty much whatever you wanted with something like a farmhouse, then turning its outbuildings from barns, chicken houses and cowsheds into delightful holiday rentals was absolutely off-limits.

All to do with local zoning and planning rules, and honestly not worth even attempting to explain, save to say that our plan for turning a farm into a holiday destination was a non-negotiable, non-starter.

And how did we find this out ? We finally came across an agent who told us the truth !

Ironically, we'd been so used to hearing the 'incorrect version' of the story, that our initial reaction on first hearing the 'correct version' was that this was mistaken ! It was only after checking things out with the local authorities that we finally got the authentic side of the story.

Bottom line is never lose sight of the basic fact that an agent's first priority is to sell property at the best price they can get for the current owner. Not to get you the best possible deal, or give you 100% guarantees you'll be able to make any changes, or use it for whatever purpose you want.

As was the case in the UK, and also is in Italy, while an agent can't deliberately misrepresent the property being sold by claiming it's something it isn't; or mislead you by claiming the property's in sound condition when in fact it's not, they're under no obligation to provide information about the validity of any plans you might have.

Caveat emptor. Let the buyer beware !

So at the very least, you should take steps to have it independently confirmed the property you like is sound – or if it isn't, the scale and likely cost of any repair or renovation. And, again independently, seek assurances that any changes you plan to make to the property - or any holiday lettings business you plan to run – are acceptable to the local authorities.

Unless the country in which you're hoping to buy operates something like a sealed bids system for property purchase, be prepared to haggle over the price and don't be afraid of walking away if you think you're being asked to pay too much.

The C-Word...and The P-Word...

Unless you're very, *very* lucky, you're not going to find a property that meets 100% of the criteria you've set for your perfect holiday rental and home. And when that moment comes, you're going to have to..

Compromise and Prioritise
If you take a look again at what we've covered in this section, you'll know all about the key issues that should govern your property-buying choice. But what to do if there's something on the check-list that just can't be ticked ?

My own view is that the only real set-in-stone, non-negotiable issue is the supreme importance of buying a property with the WOW ! factor. You should find that all the other important-to-you considerations will then fall into place on your list.

Aside from that vital WOW ! factor, you'll find,

* there'll probably be a few other 'must-have' priorities on your list about which you won't want to compromise at all.

- perhaps a few more items you're prepared to be little more relaxed about. Great if the majority can be ticked – but not a complete deal-breaker if one or two can't be.

- maybe then quite a few considerations you'd class as 'pretty important', but as long a decent number are met, you won't be too fussed if some of them aren't.

- and finally, a handful of odds-and-ends you'd regard as, "Not the end of the world if we have to live without."

The only real problem will arise if one – or more – of your absolute must-have's aren't available. Then you might have some serious thinking to do.

Otherwise, it's just a case of balancing what *is* available in your proposed property purchase with what *isn't,* and compromising accordingly. And as with all else here, try and put the needs of your future guests above your own.

This doesn't mean that your own home should be in the basement, while your guests enjoy the penthouse. Nor the other way round.

Compromise...

When you can step back, happy in the knowledge that all the prioritised factors on your list have been satisfactorily lined-up - plus as many as possible of all the others; and you're easy with having sensibly compromised where that's been necessary – that's the moment to go ahead and sign on the dotted line.

However..there is one final option that might appeal to you...

As we found ourselves during our own experiences at this stage of our plans, the entire process of property hunting and subsequent renovation/repair can take time.

But there is a kind of all-in, one-stop alternative to the multi-stage process of finding the right property for your new holiday rentals business; setting it up how you want it – and finally starting to make a living.

Your Property And Your Business – Another Option

That option – to put it simply – is to buy an existing rentals business.

Why should you consider this ? Because it's about time and money.

Once you've chosen the best area for you to live and start your business, think for a moment about the timetable you'll be locked-into before you welcome your first guest.

- You have to find the right property in the right location. Unlike where you live now, you won't be able to go property-hunting after work or at weekends. Instead, you'll need to think about booking flights, hotels and rental cars, and perhaps using up your holiday/vacation entitlement by taking time off work to go looking. So it may two or three trips spread over up to 6 months before you find what you want.

- And once you've zeroed-in on the perfect place, allow what could be several months for the various legalities and sales formalities to be completed.

- If your chosen property needs any sort of renovation/rebuilding, the work involved could take up time too. Up to a year – maybe even a little longer.

- And even if your new property needs only basic cosmetic work, that could still take 3 months or so.

- Then your new business finally opens its doors. And while – yes – you'll now be earning money, as with any new venture, it's going to take some time for your business to get fully established.

    Again from our own experience, you need to allow a good couple of years for this to happen.

- Add all that up and you'll see it'll be something like three or four years before – if all goes well – your financial plans have really bedded-down and are beginning to deliver as you hoped they would.

In the meantime though – the question again arises about what are you going to live on ?

Here's what we found...

- Between October 2007, when we arrived in Italy, and August 2009, when we had our first paying guests, our total income was precisely – nothing.

- That was 22 months - though remember we built from scratch - and while that's quick, our builders still broke records. In 2010, our second season, we did OK – but still weren't completely financially self-sufficient. In 2011 we'd just about started to get things on an even keel.

- And to get us through that, in the first period, we lived completely off capital – and then used our ever-dwindling nest-egg to top-up our rental income for the next couple of years.

- This was all actually OK, because we'd allowed for just this eventuality in our financial projections – but even so, there's a considerable stress factor when reality kicks in and you're sitting in a strange country; wondering if you've made the right decision; hoping your build will be finished on time – and that people will want to come and stay there when it is.

The alternative, once you've decided where you want to live and run your business, is to hunt-out a going concern that's up for sale. As with regular domestic properties, business owners place their properties with agents too, so once again, it's a case of spreading out the search net both on the ground and online – and seeing what materialises.

Checking off the pros and cons...

- If you decide to buy an established rentals business, you may not find one to fit the bill in your preferred location...

- ...nor set-up in the way you might have chosen yourself....

- ...nor catering for a clientele you might have chosen yourself.

- You won't have the same opportunity of putting your own 'stamp' on either your new home – or the way your new business operates – as you'd be able to do if starting from scratch.

- On the other hand, there'll be a tremendous amount of setting-up work – pretty much the entire contents of this section (and a lot of the next !) – that you won't have to do, because it'll already have been done and dusted.

- Unlike a start-up, you'll be making money from a newly-acquired going concern from Day 1 of your ownership.

- You'll need to go into the financial side of buying a going concern in very careful detail, balancing up the cost of buying, renovating and/or refurbishing a property; factoring-in all the setting-up costs you're about to discover in the next section; and setting aside enough for your day-to-day living expenses while your new business becomes established – and seeing how they compare to the one-off cost, (which won't be cheap), of acquiring somewhere that's already up-and-running.

- Essentially, by buying an 'off the shelf' solution, you'll be saving up to 75% of the time it might otherwise have taken to get a new business started...and then reach the same level that an established business might already have reached.

Don't forget the the key checks you need to make before buying a going concern...

- How long has the business been trading ?

73

- Why are the current owners selling ?

- What's the trading history going back at least three years ?

- Is there confirmation from an independent accountant and/or local tax office that all taxes currently due have been paid ?

- If a trading/operating licence is required for the business – does it have one ?

- What are the average annual outgoings ?

- How is the business currently marketed ?

- Is the full inventory of guest accommodation furnishing, fittings and equipment included in the price ?

- What else needed/in use for running the business is included in the price ?

Finally, perhaps the most important question of all...

- Disregarding everything else, will you be able to commit to running a business that someone else has started and established, with the same drive and purpose you'd bring to a business you'd started and were establishing yourself ?

If the answer is "No" or "I'm not sure" - don't do it.

I mention the idea of taking over an existing business because for some – it *is* an attractive proposition; and it *is* worth considering. On the other hand, the whole process of deciding where to move; the property hunt; renovation or rebuilding; setting everything up; and finally running the business, are all part of the...not exactly *fun*...but part of of the life-changing experience.

But unless you've taken the short-cut of buying a going concern, then regardless of the route you've taken to deciding where you actually want to move to; and finding the property you think will be just right not only for your rental guests, but for you too – the next step will be to get your holiday rentals business up and running...

3. STARTING YOUR BUSINESS

Section 3 is the longest section of this book, because there really are an awful lot of strands that need to be meshed together in the set-up stages before you can start welcoming your first guests. So along the way, you're going to be fitting out your rental property; introducing your new business to the world; and perhaps even taking your very first bookings !

We'll be covering:

- Making money from your rentals – and how to get paid

- Choosing a name for your business

- Deciding how to market your property

- Setting-up a website

- Keeping in touch – your phone and e-mail

- Getting to grips with Google and Social Media

- Fitting-out your rental. What you'll really need – and what you really won't

- The last thing to do before you open for business...

Making Money From Your Rentals

In the previous section, I mentioned the importance of deciding how many rental units you plan to be letting out – and the income you'll be hoping to make.

Clearly, money's an issue of crucial importance, so let's start this section by taking a look at how the number of rental units you have can enable you to achieve your targets.

For the purpose of illustration, let's assume you've carefully gone through your budgets; added-up the sums, and worked out you'll need your rental property to give you a gross, pre-tax income of 30,000 a year. (And whether that's £, or $, or € - or whatever - really isn't important in this exercise).

Divided by 52 weeks, 30,000 a year works out at 577 per week in round figures. But of course your rental's not going to be continuously 100% occupied from January 1 through to December 31 each and every year.

(And if it is, I'm going to ask you to finish this book...)

So the next question is – what sort of occupancy rate can you reasonably expect over the course of a year ? And that's a tough question to answer...

Holiday letting occupancy rates vary wildly from country-to-country; and from area-to-area within those countries.

The only way you're going to get anything like an accurate picture of occupancy rates in your chosen destination is to see how your likely competitors are doing – and at the same time, what they're charging.

I know some people might find this a little sneaky , but I promise you that once you've arrived and started your own business, your competitors will be keeping a very close eye on you too.

Before choosing an area for your own business, there are a number of steps you'll need to take:

- look carefully at what's already in the market-place and how many rentals (if any) are currently offering what you plan to offer

- at the same time, see what rental accommodation is available – and the rates being charged

- research how existing local accommodation is being marketed...

- ...and whether a reasonable amount of bookings are being taken both inside and outside the main holiday season.

Only by running the rule over an existing market will you be able to identify any gaps you can fill yourself; or if there are none, just weighing-up what other accommodation providers are doing and working out how to do it better – or differently.

As I mentioned earlier, we homed-in on southern Abruzzo as a good place to think about starting our own business as a result of what we turned-up in researching the rental properties already operating in the region.

- We did this through big worldwide holiday rental agencies like *TripAdvisor* and *HomeAway* - and seeing what came up on Google searches.

- In addition to discovering how many of these rental providers were around – and whereabouts in the region they were – it was also straightforward to check-out their individual availability calendars and the rentals that were being charged.

- That in turn allowed us to get a decent idea of average occupancy rates – and based on those, it was then easy enough to work out the likely financial returns.

- Using rentals in Abruzzo as a model, a good occupancy rate across the year would be around 30% - balanced between a highly achievable 90%+ in summer, down to literally 0% in the middle of winter

Doing the maths, 30% of 52 weeks is roughly 16 weeks. Divide that into your desired gross annual return of 30,000 and you get a basic average weekly rate of 1875.

Clearly, as you can't expect to charge the same in February as you do in August, you'll adjust that basic rate so it's higher in summer; lower in winter; and somewhere in-between in spring and autumn.

(Up to you whether you decide to increase your rates at Christmas, New Year, Easter and public holidays. At *Villasfor2* we don't, because when we were looking for places to stay ourselves, we found these price hikes incredibly irritating. But it's a personal call, and entirely your decision.)

So...when you look at that basic rate of 1875, two things should strike you...

- The first is that if you're to rent to groups, though at first sight 1875 might seem a high price for a week's occupancy, it's certainly not an unrealistic target.

- For a group of – say – 10 adults, 187 a week each would be an absolute bargain. That's good news, because even if that basic rate goes up by 50% in high summer – (and correspondingly *down* by 50% in the depths of winter) - it's *still* going to represent a good deal.

- Furthermore, it'll remain a good deal even if you decide to make a further tweak to your rates so that kids under – say – 16 are charged less; and the very young are accommodated for free.

There's one final part of the equation to factor-in when establishing your rates, which is to make sure you're charging neither considerably less – nor considerably more – than your competitors.

- Up to 10% more - or less – than the local average for a similar property is fine.

- Less might give you a bit of an edge, especially in the first year or so while you're becoming established.

- You can get away with a little more if you genuinely and objectively feel you're offering a better-than-average product.

- Asking for too much less than the local going rates, and you run the risk of appearing low-end and a bit desperate for business.

- Asking too much simply prices you out of the market.

I said that *two* things would strike you regarding a desired average weekly rate of 1875. The first, as we've been examining, shouldn't present a problem if you're going to be catering for groups of 10 – or more - contained in one rental unit.

The second point comes into play if your one rental unit is occupied by fewer people, because 1875 – which remember is going to be higher in summer - is going to be much harder to achieve. For only one rental unit designed for just one couple, it would be a virtual impossibility – even if you're *incredibly* high-end. For four people - feasible. For six – much easier.

However, when dealing with small capacity rental units, prospects improve greatly if you have two or more rental units. Based purely on my own local research, it seems clear that two or three smaller rental units are more profitable than a single larger one.

We have three just-for-couples units, which at peak occupancy in high summer can out-earn all but super-luxury properties holding many more than the maximum six people we can accommodate at any one time.

The outlines above of course are only illustrative figures, based on a *highly* variable set of assumptions. Nevertheless, they should give you a basic idea of where to start when working out what to charge, and as I've just mentioned, from the outset, you really won't go too far wrong if you let yourself be guided by what's being charged elsewhere locally. You'll have plenty of opportunities for adjustment once your business has become established.

As regards different price bands for different times of the year, my own view is that too many starts getting a little complicated and unwieldy. We work with just four price bands at *Villasfor2*:

- Late Spring – from early May to late June

- Summer – from late June to mid-September

- Autumn – from mid-September to late October

- Winter/Early Spring – late October – early May

Based on the illustration I gave you based on a desired target income of 30,000 a year, you can play around to your heart's content with higher – or lower – targets to go for in your first year and see how they'd relate to the weekly rentals you'd have to charge, (and more importantly – achieve) – and how realistic those rental charges might be.

When you've finally decide on weekly rates for your first year, don't be afraid of bringing them down a little if the initial trade isn't quite what you'd hoped. There's no law that says you can't change your rates mid-season, but only do it once a year – and then by not more than around 5%.

How to get paid !
Once you've decided how much to charge, the next step will be deciding how your guests will actually pay you for their holidays.

If you're taking bookings through a rentals listing agency, you have no choice about how this happens. Your guests will pay the agency for the full cost of their stay; the agency will then deduct their commission; and you'll get paid the balance.

(The time-frame in which this happens is often a sore point between the bigger agencies and owners. Like you, agencies will ask for payment several weeks before a guest's arrival date – but they don't actually release whatever's due to you until a day or two after the guest has checked-in.

In contrast – and going purely by our own experiences – smaller agencies are generally very good about passing on your money in reasonable time before guests arrive).

If you plan on taking bookings through your own website, you'll of course save on agency fees. We'll soon be going through the mechanics of actually taking a booking, but for now we'll just be covering the options open to you for accepting direct payments.

And they come down to cash - (which includes bank transfers and cheques as well as money in your hand) – or credit cards

Cash
At its most basic, this involves nothing more than the guest handing over a pile of banknotes on arrival. It's the simplest form of payment – and let's face it, for a whole host of reasons, people like getting paid in cash – and you might be no exception.

And while you might over the years happily take in cash payments without any mishaps, unfortunately, as far as holiday rentals are concerned, it's also the payment method open to the most problems...

A couple of examples...

- you've agreed the cost of your guest's stay in advance, But on arrival, they suddenly start finding fault with your rental.

- They don't like this...or that. *This* isn't as described on your site...and *that's* simply wrong. It's all *very* disappointing...but...they've nowhere else to go – and don't have much option other than to stay – but they're certainly *not* going to pay the agreed price when *so* much is at fault.

  You'll be offered much less. And you'll all know they have you over a barrel. Yes – you can insist they pay the full amount or leave. But then you'll get nothing. So you swallow your pride; take what's offered; and chalk it up to experience.

- Or - your guest arrives with no money at all...

- They're *really* sorry, but they figured they'd get a better exchange rate once they were here, rather than back home...and don't worry, because *first thing* in the morning, they'll be off to the bank to get what's needed out of the ATM.

Except...they'll then discover a mysterious problem has developed with their card, which'll take a day or two to get sorted out. (They might offer to pay by credit card at this point, being savvy enough to know that small owner-renters like you generally don't have the facilities to accept on-site card payments).

This will all be be spun-out for as long as they think they can get away with it, then one morning, you'll find they've gone – and you haven't been paid a penny. Did you take a note of their car registration number when they arrived so you can pass it on to the police ? No – probably not... You might have taken a photocopy of their passports, but in this kind of situation, that's next to useless.

- No, we haven't fallen victim to these two little scams – though other owners have – but we *have* had similar ruses tried out on us, which thankfully (so far) haven't taken us in.

Bottom line is that – for me at any rate - cash can be too much of a problem. And so are cheques. If one is sent to you in in good time, and can be cleared before a guest's arrival; and if it's in the same currency as the one in which you operate, it's just about OK if there are no other available options. But otherwise – No. Once again, the process is too open to abuse. Same goes for wire services.

The only acceptable, reasonably safe, and regularly-used form of cash payment is by online money transfer. If both you and your guest have secure internet home banking facilities capable of transferring funds internationally, then it's certainly an option, though once again, ensure that the amount in question has been cleared and credited to your account before confirming the booking.

Cards
Online shopping is such an everyday activity now, that when it comes to paying for their holiday, your guests will be surprised if you *don't* accept cards. (And for the sake of this exercise, I'm taking here about

both credit cards *and* bank payment cards).

In fact, because using a card is so quick, easy and convenient, you could well lose the odd booking if your preferred payment method is by something relatively slow and time-consuming like a money transfer, rather than a card transaction that can be instantly completed in a couple of clicks.

(A bank transfer takes a few days to arrive and be cleared. A confirmed card transaction takes a few seconds. And when your potential guest also wants to get on with the rest of their holiday arrangements and get them wrapped up asap, any delay can be an absolute deal-breaker).

Only problem about cards is that the major providers like Visa, MasterCard and Amex will be highly unlikely to set you up with the necessary facilities for you to accept online payments.

There'll be two main reasons for this: as far as their transaction commission payments are concerned, you won't generate anywhere near an acceptable volume of business to make dealing with you worth their while; and you won't have the deep levels of electronic security on your home computer system necessary to prevent card abuse.

An alternative to dealing direct with a card provider is what's known as a card-processing company. These provide the necessary software and/or programs for you to accept card payments on your website, but instead of dealing directly with the card provider, payments are then channelled through the card-processing company, who of course take a fee and/or commission in the process.

In my experience however, these companies too aren't generally enthusiastic about taking on a business like a holiday rental which is going to generate a comparatively small number of annual transactions.

Happily, the only other option open to you for accepting card payments is also – in my view – by some way the best.

That's PayPal.

You may currently have a personal PayPal account of your own for online shopping. In any event, you'll almost certainly have heard of them – and so will your guests - which is important, as it's a trusted global brand.

If you *do* already have a personal PayPal account, it's easy enough to upgrade this to a Business Account – and you're good to go.

- The commission rate you pay is low – a little over 3%, plus a small transaction fee

- It's fast – and free to use for your guest

- It accepts funds in practically every currency available on the planet

- Your rental fees are available to you the instant a guest has paid

- And there's no necessity for your guest to have, or open, a PayPal account to use the service.

A little important admin work...
In addition to working out your weekly rates - and arranging how your guests can pay - there are also a couple of other bits of setting-up admin work you'll need to take care of around now.

Pay a visit to your local authorities – with whom you're hopefully on good terms after your previous contacts with them – and check whether your new rentals venture needs any form of operating licence, or official approval. Check too what kind of information – if any – you'll be expected to collect about your guests and/or any paperwork they'll need to sign on their arrival.

You may find you also need the ability to photocopy passports/ID documents – and possibly fax these to your country's law-enforcement authorities. (A printer that can also fax, scan and copy documents is perfect for this.)

Additionally, do seek out a good local accountant or tax consultant who can advise you about likely tax liabilities – and the financial records you'll need to keep as the basis on which these can be calculated.

Best to take care of these factors well before you open for business. If you *do* need some kind of licence, there may be a wait before this is issued; while – again speaking from our own experience – settling on exactly the right tax model on which we'd be running *Villasfor2,* though reasonably straightforward, did take a little time.

Introducing Yourself To The World

We're now at the point where you've found and bought the perfect holiday rental property in the location of your dreams. Work is just about to start on doing whatever you think is necessary to provide your guests with a great base for their holiday; and for you and your family, a lovely home in which to live for many happy years.

In the 'set-up timetable' a few pages back, I reckoned that this stage of getting your new place ready would take three months or so for any basic redecoration/cosmetic repair work; and up to a year - or maybe longer - for more serious renovation/rebuilding.

During this period, *you're* going to be working flat-out to establish your presence in the holiday rentals market (and more...), because the idea is for you to finish *your* side of the work at about the same time as the builders finish *theirs* – and you can then formally open for business.

If you leave the setting-up too long, you might find the builders have finished and gone, leaving you with a highly rentable – and empty – holiday property that nobody knows about.

As far as is realistically possible, the building and set-up work should finish together.

Setting your opening date...

Giving yourself a target to work towards will focus everyone's mind perfectly ! Impress upon your builders that the date you choose is the day you open for business – *not* the target day for them to finish work. In reality, you want the builders cleared-up and gone at least a month before you open, which in turn gives you a reasonable amount of time to get your rentals furnished and ready to receive guests.

(It's not important whether you actually *do* have guests arriving on your 'official' opening day or not. Getting your accommodation ready to a deadline will be very good practice for what you *will* be doing for real soon enough, and you need to develop a mindset and a way of working to ensure that whenever guests arrive, everything is ready for them.

Clean. Fresh. Welcoming.

Not, "Oops...sorry...we haven't quite finished. Can you go and get a coffee and come back in an hour ?"

There can be a degree of flexibility about your your starting date. If yours is primarily going to be a summertime rental, there's not much point in riding your builders hard to finish before Christmas. On the other hand, for a summer rental. it's not unreasonable to set May 1 as your start date and then, (allowing for the usual inevitable over-run), impressing on your builders you want them out sometime in March.

Don't be too discouraged though if your builders tell you there's genuinely no way they're going to finish until June/July. That's exactly what happened to us, and while we were frustrated, annoyed, and disappointed at first by the news - feeling in some way that our first summer season was being 'wasted' - as it turned out, it was no bad thing.

Here's the positive spin...

Your first season will be the most important, testing and unforgiving period you'll probably ever have running your new business. You may not have many guests during your first season – but you will have some – and the experience they have staying with you will be reflected in any reviews they might submit to sites like *TripAdvisor*, *Trust Pilot* and *Yelp*.

If anything goes wrong with any stay during your first season, that could well trigger a lukewarm, or downright unfavourable, review – which won't get your new business off to the best of starts.

Into your second season and beyond, when hopefully you'll already have a few 5-star reviews to your credit, the very occasional bad one won't do you too much harm. But starting with critical comments before you've taken in any good ones could put a few potential guests off, and take some recovery time to put right.

All this isn't made any easier by the fact that your debut season is the time you're likeliest to make mistakes. You'll probably be very nervous to start with, wondering if your first guests are enjoying their holiday – and as with any new and unfamiliar job, before you really learn how to do it well, accidents can happen.

And the longer your first season, the greater the likelihood of that. So if your set-up isn't finished by the time you'd hoped, don't regard it as an opportunity lost. Think of whatever time *is* available for 'Season 1' as an easy introduction to your new career, and the challenges that lie ahead.

On our own project in Abruzzo, the builders finally vacated the site in late June. Being aware for some time previously that this was going to happen, we built in a week or two of 'buffer time' to cover the possibility of any over-run – and set August 1 in 2009 as our opening date.

The build-up to that of course was a bit like when you decide to hold a party. You send out invitations - and then start to worry if anyone's going to come !

I think we set our August 1 opening date back in January 09, and though it took a few weeks - and after our first few enquiries had come to nothing - you can imagine how we felt when we finally secured our very first booking – and the money that came with it !

That initial booking was for a week in mid-August. Five more bookings followed for later in August and September; then one apiece in October, November and December. So by the time the year ended, we'd welcomed nine sets of guests – which was in fact a fairly manageable and straightforward introduction to our new business.

Though August and September had been quite busy, the fact that it was just for a few weeks made it so much easier. Less time to make any beginners' mistakes (there *were* a few, but thankfully nothing career-destroying); less time to become overwhelmed by coping with a new job in unfamiliar surroundings over the course of a full summer season; and more time to start getting the hang of what we were actually trying to do - and getting to grips with how to do it.

By the time we finally came up for air, we had our first good reviews; a far more realistic (and a bit less rose-tinted) idea of what running a holiday rentals business actually entailed; the confidence that – yes – we can do this ! And plenty of time to put these new experiences to use in planning our second season.

Choosing your business name

It was Shakespeare who originally asked, "What's in a name ?" and when it comes to deciding what to call your new holiday rentals business, the answer is - "Quite a lot"...

Do you actually *need* a business name ? Personally - Yes. I think you do.

To explain why, take a quick flick through any set of holiday rental listings on the internet, and the ones that really stand out are those with good names.

- "Amazing holiday villa. Near beach. Stunning views. Sleeps 6" isn't a name – it's a description.

- Can you answer the phone by saying, "Hi ! This is amazing holiday villa. Near beach. Stunning views. Sleeps 6 speaking..." ?

89

- Can you get "Amazing holiday villa. Near beach. Stunning views. Sleeps 6" on a business card ?

- Or when you meet someone and are telling them what you do for a living, can you say, "Oh...I run a vacation rental called Amazing holiday villa. Near beach. Stunning views. Sleeps 6" ?

No. You can't.

Exercise a little creativity and ingenuity by summing up your property and/or what you do there in just a handful of words.

Villasfor2 tells you exactly what kind of holiday accommodation we offer.

For your rental property, depending on who you see as your target audience, it might be something along the lines of – say - *KidsWelcomeHolidays*.

You can tie your property to a geographical location - *Our Place in Calabria*.

Or maybe get inspiration from a local landmark; wildlife, plants or trees that may thrive in the area; or simply just what you can see out of the window - *Oceanview Rentals*.

Names in the country's language can be fine – like *Casa del Sol* for example – but anything that's not immediately understandable rather misses the point.

As with any business name, yours will need to be to-the-point, punchy and easy to remember. When you've come up with something great - run it through a Google search to see if anyone else is using it.

Whatever name you go for, you can then add a brief qualifying phrase, which might sit happily on an email signature - (*Villasfor2's* is "The Italy Villa Holiday For Couples") - a letterhead, brochure, or website.

And once you've chosen your business name, it'll be time to start getting it out there into the holiday rentals marketplace, and taking the first steps in selling yourself...

How do I do that ?

It depends very simply on how you primarily plan to market your holiday rental property.

If the idea is to rely heavily on lettings agencies for your guests, then a website – if you choose to have one – need be little more than an expanded brochure. And *provided* the agencies do a good job for you, it probably wouldn't matter greatly if you decided to do without a site altogether.

Or you might see a website as your key, front-line marketing tool to actively generate bookings. If that's the case however – and it was certainly our own initial marketing choice – then you need to be absolutely aware of the commitment a site will demand from you. It's anything but a 'set-and-forget' add-on.

Let's take a look at the plus and minus points of both options...

Using A Lettings Agency

If you haven't come across big international agencies like *TripAdvisor Rentals* or *HomeAway* before, take a long look at their websites to see what they do and how they do it. And you'll also come across innumerable smaller agencies specialising in area-specific lettings around the world.

By doing this, you'll get a feel of what potential renters see when they're looking for somewhere to book for their holidays. You'll also notice which listings stand out – and which don't. And why...

To list your own property on any of these sites is generally very easy, though you do need a few basic computer skills.

- All lettings sites I've come across and used myself, operate on the same principles in that listing your property will be free – (though some *do* levy a charge for prime positions in their listings) - and you can list with as many lettings agencies as you like.

- Using a (usually) very simple template, you'll upload photographs and descriptions of your property, together with your rental prices. (Which is where you'll need some basic computer know-how to do this).

- You'll also have an availability calendar as part of your listing on which potential guests can see when you're free – and you can mark dates as unavailable when you're booked .

If this all seems like a pretty good deal, there is of course a downside. These agencies aren't charities, and while they'll allow you to list for free, they'll charge a commission on any booking they obtain for you. This can vary from 3-10% for the bigger international agencies, up to 15/20/25% for smaller, local companies.

I'm reasonably easy with even the higher commission rates – though I've steered-clear of those asking for 25%. On the basis that any agency booking is one I probably wouldn't otherwise have got, I tend to regard these as a bonus to add to those generated by the *Villasfor2* website.

Consequently – when considering the resulting commission payments – I take the view that getting 80% of something is better than getting 100% of nothing.

Of course you may be slightly less sanguine about this if agency bookings are your sole source of income...

There are however a couple of key areas where even the best lettings agencies don't score highly. It's all to do with the visibility of your listing.

The more listings featured on any agency website for wherever you happen to be based, the more you're in danger of becoming just another face in the crowd – just another holiday rental listing on page, after page, after page of them.

Consequently you'll need some real attention-grabbing photographs -

plus a sales pitch to match - to make your place stand out.

You can also find your property buried well away from the first two or three pages of listings, which - despite assertions otherwise – are all that potential guests ever really go through in detail before each rental property starts looking the same.

It's true that while many agencies do their best to be fair by employing complicated algorithms to try and ensure every listing gets a bit of time on page 1, for some that'll be at times of the day when there's likely to be peak interest – and for others, it'll be at 3am...

But once again - to give most agencies their due – through the means of various search options on their sites, they'll enable the casual browser to specify pretty exactly the kind of holiday they're looking for. So if you in turn have set-out crisply and clearly the attractions and amenities at your own rental, the better chance you have of being found in an online search.

The big plus of these holiday property agencies is that the biggest, most-visited, and most-established international sites will pull-in infinitely more viewing hits than your own website – if you have one – can ever hope to achieve.

The big minus is that if you *don't* have a website of your own, you'll be virtually 100% reliant on agencies for your bookings.

Your Own Website

I have to confess that for me, the whole *'website vs no website'* argument is an absolute no-brainer. Right from the start, the *Villasfor2* website has been vital to the way we market our business and attract customers, to the extent that in any given year, something like 55-65% of all bookings we take will be generated from the site.

And while – yes – we *do* use lettings agencies as well, the fact we're not totally reliant on them for our income allows us to be selective as to which we use/don't use.

In turn, because most of our bookings come to us directly, it means we save on lettings agency commissions – which of course means more money for us !

But I also have to confess that running a successful site takes money to start – and time to continue. It very definitely is an everyday commitment.

About the only set of circumstances I can think of that *doesn't* require you to give constant attention to your site, is if it's set-up as nothing much more than a glorified brochure for your business. A website with good photographs and well-written copy, which basically allows you to expand on the – by necessity – fairly brief information that an agency listings site allows you to provide, will need minimal attention.

And as I mentioned above, if you're happy with the level of business a listings agency is pulling in, there's really no need for a website at all.

In fact, based on the entirely unscientific evidence of my own personal observation, I'd say that the majority of holiday rentals *don't* have their own dedicated website.

So if that's true – why bother with a website at all ? The answer is that it gives you so much more control over your business.

On a listings agency site, you'll be in competition with a great many other rental business owners, all hungry to secure bookings. As all listings on the site will have been generated by using the same agency template, they'll all conform to strict limitations regarding the number of photographs that can be featured, and how many words that are allowed to 'sell' rentals.

Within those confines, some listings will have,

- better quality and/or more eye-catching pictures than you do.

- others will have a skilful way with words that describe their property and the type of holidays they offer, that you maybe don't.

- There'll be those that offer better value and more/better amenities than you.

- Or are easier to get to.

- Or have more/better reviews.

In turn though, *your* listing will hopefully make other owners think about what *you* might be doing/offering that *they* aren't.

In short – it's all about competition. It's about forcing someone looking through the listings to decide whether they want to go on holiday to Property A. Or B. Or maybe C. Or D (which looks great). Or E, F. Perhaps G (the cheapest of them all), or H.

It's confusing.

On your own website, there's no competition. It's just you. And you'll stand or fall by how enticing you can make what you're offering.

More subtly, it's also about reducing choice from any number of possibilities to just one. Instead of forcing someone to choose one of several available – and broadly similar – options, as would be the case on a listings agency site, your own dedicated site allows you to ask a completely different and much simpler question:

"Would you like to come here for your holiday ?"

Or, even better, "You *would* like to come here for your holiday - wouldn't you ?"

Yes...or No...

And if your site's doing its job properly, it'll be – Yes.

So – how do you go about putting together the kind of website that'll give your business this kind of boost ?

That's where the outlay in terms of time and money comes in. A really effective site needs to be up-and-running before your business opens, (to generate interest and bookings), and once it's live and online – though the annual financial costs are then low – it will require virtually daily input from you to run at optimum levels.

Here's a checklist of the first steps that need to be taken...

- Initially, you'll need to come up with a domain name – like *Villasfor2.com* – that reflects your business. Buying a domain name isn't expensive – and neither is the annual 'ownership fee' you'll need to pay as long as you want the site. (And you can pay for several years at a time up-front).

- Provided nobody's thought of your chosen domain name beforehand, you can easily buy and register it online with one of many international specialist companies offering this service. You'll easily find these with a Google search. (I've used *GoDaddy* before and found it just fine.)

- There's a chance you might find that '*yourchosenname.com*' has already been registered. But if that's the case, '*yourchosenname.net*', or – if you're looking to primarily attract British guests - '*yourchosenname.co.uk*' might still be up for grabs.

  There's now a vast choice of available suffixes – but *.com* sites are still the ones that really carry the most international online clout and it's the suffix to go for if you can.

Congratulations ! Without too much time and effort – or money ! - you have a legally-registered domain ! Now you need the actual website to go with it...

There are basically two ways to about this: Do it yourself; or pay a Website Designer to do it for you.

D-I-Y isn't the technical near-impossibility it once used to be, as there's been a big improvement in the user-friendliness and accessibility of the assorted software and programs you'll need to get your site active.

But that said, it's still not a task to be attempted lightly unless you really do have a better-than-average grasp of the necessary computer skills.

It's true however that if you intend just making your site a pumped-up brochure for your rental, things get a lot easier, and a bit of time online should find you a simple 'walk-you-through-the-process' app that'll allow you achieve this.

On the other hand – especially bearing in mind all the other things you'll be coping with at this stage of your project – the easiest, least-stressful, and probably more reliable course of action will be to hire a Website Designer.

- What does a Designer do ? A good one will discuss with you what you actually want your site to achieve - probably reining-in some of your less practical ideas and suggesting a few alternatives – and then basically 'building' the site from the ground up.

- A less-good Designer might be more concerned with shoe-horning your site into a tried-and-tested theme they're happy working with. Which might be good for them – but perhaps not for you.

- Best course of action will be to talk a handful of Designers to see how you get on with them - and go through samples of their work, looking at the practicality and effectiveness of the sites they've designed just as much as their eye-appeal.

- Getting your site off the ground should ideally be just the start of a long-term relationship you'll have with your Designer.

Underlining the fact that websites aren't 'set-and-forget',

- software can become out-of-date

- aspects of your site can - for no apparent reason - simply stop working

- at some point, you'll want to refresh and update your site's appearance.

In these instances, it's always best to use your original Designer, who'll know their way round your site better than anyone else.

I really wish at this point I could give you some idea about the cost of creating your website, but even taking the UK alone – which is the start and finish of my own experience – fees do vary considerably even from one part of the country to another.

Factoring-in what Designers charge elsewhere in the world, together with how simple or complex your site is going to be, make it impossible – and inadvisable - to pass on even a ballpark cost guideline.

However, even just talking to three or four designers will give you an idea of the going-rate for your job, and will enable you to spot if anyone is loading their fees.

- This is such an important project that for ease of communication, it's vital you choose to work with someone with whom you have a first language in common.

- At this stage, you might well have moved to a new country, but – as I've found myself – it's now so easy to talk face-to-face with someone online, it really doesn't matter where you – or they – actually live.

Aside from constructing and maintaining your website then, what else does a Designer do ?

- If you don't already have one, they'll fix you up with a web hosting company. Their place in this jigsaw is to provide the necessary technicalities for your site to go online – and stay there.

- Some registration companies from whom you bought your domain name provide a one-stop service for web hosting too, so you might already have taken care of this.

- A designer will also choose what's known as a 'Content Management System' for your site. This basically is a computer program that takes all the words, pictures and everything else you want to appear on your website and then ensures the right words appear with the right pictures on the right pages, and that your entire site simply 'works'.

- The CMS will ensure that anyone who logs onto your site can easily navigate their way round its component pages – and if needs be, to interact with you, by getting the information they need to decide whether or not to make a booking.

- And once they've made that decision, *how* to make a booking.

- *Villasfor2* runs on a very popular and widely-used Content Management System, called *Wordpress*. There are several alternative options to this program, and your Designer will have one they favour.

They'll also show you how to use your CMS, which you'll need to know for simple tasks like,

- ensuring your Availability Calendar and rental rates are up-to-date.

- Taking care of any necessary copy rewrites...

- ...or swapping one photo for another on a particular page,

- plus more complex tasks, as you become more confident and experienced.

These initial day-to-day tasks aren't that difficult to either learn or carry out – once you've seen for yourself how straightforward they are, they shouldn't hold any fears for you.

Talking of a Content Management System of course assumes there is 'content' for it to 'manage'. So the next question is, who's going to produce the words and pictures that'll be used on your site ?

Once again, the answer is D-I-Y – or get someone else to do it...

- If you opt for the latter course of action, the first person to ask about someone to write content for your site is your site designer. If they don't know of anyone – or if you haven't used a designer - Google-search "find web content writer" - and spend some time looking at what comes up !

- Of course, you'll need to pay for this and you'll get exactly what you pay for in terms of the quality of the result.

- You'll need to spend considerable care briefing your writer about *exactly* what you want on each page of your site, because the closer you can get to an acceptable result at the first or second shot will reduce the need for expensive/extensive re-writes.

- While not denying the talents of many web content writers, I have to say that the only person who can *really* write from the heart in describing your holiday rentals is you. So at the very least – give it a try...and get those who'll be working with you on this project to help.

- If you can capture in words the excitement and enthusiasm you feel for your new venture, I promise this'll come across to anyone reading it. And if you can also get over your passion and commitment for providing memorable holidays, you'll have achieved more than even the most skilled content writer.

- I have to acknowledge that because I'd spent my entire working life as a journalist before starting *Villasfor2*, writing the necessary copy for our site was a fairly straightforward task for me. That was a lucky break – but it certainly doesn't mean you have to be a professional – or pay money to one – to produce words for your site which are absolutely fine.

- To encourage you further, the great thing about a website is that it actually doesn't *need* vast long essays to fill. In fact, by far the most commonly-made mistake is to write too much.

- Of much more importance is to ensure what you *do* write is error-free and grammatical. If it isn't, it creates an indelibly bad impression about you and your business.

- Always use a good word-processing program on your computer for anything you write for your site and take advantage of the 'Spelling and Grammar' tools on these programs to check your copy. Everybody always makes mistakes working on a keyboard – but nobody need look like an idiot as a result.

- At its most basic, your home page – the gateway to the rest of your site – needs nothing more than one really great picture to grab attention, and then literally no more than 300-400 words – or even less - to introduce your site, together with a brief outline what it's all about.

- The ultimate aim being to provide enough interest and promise on your home page to make your site visitor want to see what else you have to offer.

- Think for a moment about what *you* do when you're browsing the web. If you like a home page picture, you'll glance at the words alongside it. If you're then faced with great slabs of copy disappearing off the bottom of the page, you're unlikely to settle down and start wading through it. You'll skim through a few lines; get bored; give up; and click onto another site. The same goes for everyone who visits *your* site.

- But if alongside that great opening picture on a site are just a few crisp, tight, easy-to-read sentences, you might at least start to read what they have to say. And in the next few seconds (literally...) you'll have decided whether these opening words have delivered enough to keep you interested – or whether you'll click onto another page.

- And once you've got someone past that home page on *your* site, your word-count can then become a little more expansive on other pages. But on page 1, less is always more – and exactly the same principle applies when you're writing copy for a rentals agency site listing.

Important !

Regardless of whether you build your site yourself, or use a designer – or whether your site is your major sales tool, or an expanded brochure, it **must** contain two key elements:

Availability Calendar

This is what you use to keep track of all your bookings; and is what a potential guest uses to see whether you have availability on any given date. The vast majority of calendars come as a modular 'plug-in' which your designer – or you - can simply slot into an appropriate place on your site.

I know some owners don't have Availability Calendars on their websites, and instead instruct potential guests to contact them with their chosen dates – and then mail them back to tell them whether those dates are free or not. (And if they're not, to then suggest alternatives).

Personally, I think this is a bad idea, as it just gets in the way of a possible booking by adding one – or even more - completely unnecessary steps, which take both time and effort. The fact that most Calendars are free – in addition to being easy to install and maintain - makes adding one to your site is a complete no-brainer.

Your calendar's a vital and integral part of your business. We'll be talking more about it shortly...

Contact Form

There has to be a way of getting hold of you that's easy and foolproof. Initial contact's a choice of either by e-mail or phone, and the vast majority of potential guests prefer to simply drop you a line.

And the way they do this from your site is by using another (usually free) modular plug-in application. All Contact Forms will feature some type of interactive anti-spam protection to prevent your business mailbox - (more about that in a just a couple of pages) - getting swamped with rubbish.

There are so many occasions when – for a variety of reasons - a potential guest needs to drop you a line, that a simple and reliable way of doing this as part of your site – and underlining again that Contact Forms are easy to install and run - shouldn't even be a discussion point.

We've Covered The Words – Now For The Pictures !

As with other aspects of your website, you can buy-in the help of a professional photographer. Or take the pictures yourself. Don't be intimidated by this, because even if you're unsure about writing the content for your website, you should find taking any necessary photos an absolute breeze.

- I'm now going to blow away a lot of the hype surrounding taking photos for a website, because although – assuming you know how to use it properly – you'll get superb results from some high-end digital camera, you don't actually *need* one to take the kind of photo that'll look great on your site.

- Every single picture on the *Villasfor2* site was taken with a mid-range 'point-and-shoot' compact camera, usually on fully automatic setting.

- The only piece of vaguely technical advice I'd pass on is that a 16 - 20 megapixel camera will be just fine for the kind of pictures you need to take for your site.

- Any higher spec than that would be wasted overkill.

Why do I say this ? As briefly and simply as I can explain, the more megapixels a camera has, the more detail it can capture. (This also makes for better quality enlargements – though that's not really an issue here).

However, all your website photos are– by definition - going to be viewed on a desktop computer screen; or a laptop; or a tablet; or a phone. And the further down the scale you go, more of the finer details are going to be lost.

Bottom line is that for the purpose of taking pictures for your website, a 16 - 20MP camera is every bit as good as anything else.

And they're a *lot* better than smartphone cameras. Even very good and highly spec'd smartphones.

It's all about the light sensors in phone cameras, and light sensors in compact cameras, and is *way* outside the scope of this book, but just suffice it to say, a decent point-and-shoot will cost much less and take better photos for the purpose of illustrating your website than a smartphone.

If you disagree, please don't write.

Arm yourself with your compact camera, plus a high-capacity photo SD card, and on a bright, sunny, blue-sky day – (because grey skies don't make for enticing holiday rental website shots) – take yourself out and shoot literally hundreds of pictures of your rental, (both inside and out); its surroundings; local towns; sights; bars; restaurants; scenery and anything else that catches your eye.

That's the beauty of digital photography – once you've got the camera, it's basically free to use ! If your computer doesn't have one pre-loaded, download a basic photo app that'll allow you to crop/resize your pictures and make a few modest quality tweaks, and that'll be all you need to get you started.

Yes – the initial phase of building up a good library of images for your website is labour-intensive, but once it's done – it's done, and you can then basically drop into cruise-control and take pictures for fun, swapping round images on your site as the mood takes you.

For an amateur like you – and me too for that matter – the more shots you take, the better your chance of a really good one. And while you'll of course want *all* the pictures on your website to be great, only one *must* be.

The Money Shot

A few pages back, we went over **The Killer Question** that you should ask yourself when viewing any potential property purchase in the initial stages of setting up your rental business.

In its own way, The Money Shot is equally important.

What is The Money Shot ?

- It's the lead photo on your home page, and the reason it's so important is because it represents the one and only chance you'll have to grab anyone looking at your website – or rentals agency listing.

- What should The Money Shot show ? Whatever in your view is the single unique factor that sets your rental apart from the rest. Within those confines, provided it's extra-special, it can be anything you like.

- The Money Shot has to deliver on two separate counts:

- the first is obvious. A reaction from anyone seeing it of, "WOW – that looks amazing !"

- the second is the ability of your Money Shot to then prompt a follow-up reaction of, "I could just picture myself there..."

If you feel inclined, take a look at the *Villasfor2* Money Shot – (the same as we've used from day 1 – though progressively re-shot on better quality cameras !) - and I hope you'll get a similarly positive reaction to the one we know a great many of our guests have had.

As regards our shot, when a potential guest has taken in the view and our surroundings, and starts wondering which sunbed they'd choose, and thinking how inviting the pool looks, the question I hope they might then ask themselves is, "I wonder how much a couple of weeks in July would cost ?"

And we might be on the brink of a booking...

An equally attention-grabbing image of your own rental will unquestionably serve you just as well.

A little trick of the trade...
At the start of this section, we established you'd have several months – perhaps up to a year – while your property is being finished-off to get yourself set-up with a business name and decide whether you'd be marketing your property via a website...or a rentals agency listing...or both.

Bearing in mind you'll be needing lots of attractive pictures of your property and its surrounds with which to entice potential guests, you might be wondering exactly *how* you're supposed to take pictures if your property/garden/pool isn't actually ready yet.

And the answer is – be creative. Or to put it another way - cheat !

We were in exactly the same position of not having much in the way of website content/pictures before our opening – and in fact on the very first version of our site, (because we realised we had to show *something*), we ended-up showing artist's impressions of what things would be like once they were actually finished.

Not surprisingly, we didn't get a single booking from these – and thankfully, it was a very short-lived experiment until we had proper photographs to put in our site, even though some of them weren't quite all they seemed...

I'll give you an example...

It was February 2009...our site was up-and-running...and I desperately needed to include a photo of our pool.

At this point, the pool had in fact been completed – but because it hadn't yet been plumbed-in to the water supply, we hadn't been able to fill it. I tried a couple of exploratory poolside shots – and ended up with pictures of an unmistakably empty pool.

Not ideal.

So I crouched down and took as low an angle shot of the pool and accompanying sunbeds/umbrella as I could. You could see the rim of the pool – and a couple of inches of pool liner – but you couldn't see it was empty.

Perfect !

So much so in fact that we went on using the photo for quite a long time – even when the pool had been filled...

It didn't matter either that the picture was taken in February. (Because a lovely, sunny winter's day doesn't really look all that different to a lovely sunny summer's day...)

The point of this is to underline to you that you *need* images for your website/agency listing – but even if a key factor of your rental isn't quite ready when you need its picture, it's not necessarily a major issue.

Just exercise a little ingenuity...

Talking To The World – Your Phone and E-Mail

If you want to come across to your prospective guests as professional and well-run, you'll need an email address and phone number that you use exclusively for your business.

Both are quick, easy and cost very little to organise.

If you have your own website, your site designer can build-in as many dedicated email addresses for your new site as you want.

- There'll be your business's main email address – something like *enquiries@ yourchosenname.com...*

- ...and you and your family can each have your own personal address – *yourname@ yourchosenname.com; yourpartner @yourchosenname.com* – and so on.

- If you don't have your own website, then simply set-up an email account for you to use for your business with Google, or some other provider – *yourchosenname@ gmail.com.*

- Same for however many other personal business addresses you need.

Your own home will probably have a landline telephone, but for professional purposes, there'll be no way of knowing when it starts ringing, if it's about a booking in August – or a friend ringing for a chat.

Another landline isn't really the answer, because aside from the cost involved - for business purposes, you need to be available even when you're out of the house.

The solution is no more complicated or costly than getting hold of a fairly basic cellphone.

- You'll use its number - and set the ringtone - *only* for business, so the minute someone calls, you'll know instantly it's business-related – and you'll then be able to answer the call professionally - "Hi...this is XYZ Rentals – John speaking..." - as opposed to, "Hello...?"

- Not a bad idea either to load your new phone with a calendar app, so you you can see all your bookings at a glance...

- ...instantly tell a caller whether you have availability on their chosen holiday dates...

- ...and have your nightly/weekly rates on your phone too.

Granted this might mean you need to carry a personal and a business cell with you at all times – but it's something you get used to !

(You *can* also get hold of cell phones that can work with two SIM-cards – giving you two separate numbers on the same phone – which of course does away with the need for carrying two phones around.

I – briefly – tried this out at one point; found it incredibly and irritatingly fiddly; and so went back to the decidedly low-tec, two-phone option...)

Take things a stage further like we do and – by using Skype – we have a UK phone number which automatically connects UK callers to our Italian business cellphone - all for the price of a UK call.

I have absolutely no idea of the technology involved, but it works perfectly; is cheap; and is a very useful business extra.

I'm sure that aside from Skype, other communications companies offer the same or similar services on a worldwide basis.

Getting To Grips With Google

You probably know Google best as the ultimate search engine. What you might not know is that getting on with Google will form an indispensable part of your business plan – and that Google also provides (completely for free) a range of tools that let you know how well your website performs – and how you can make it do better.

Ask your site designer – or Google itself – how a program called Google Analytics works.

When you do a Google search for something, have you ever wondered how it's decided what items appear on various pages of your search results ? And in what order ? The answer is – Google decides.

On what criteria does Google base its decision ? Good question – and one to which there isn't an accurate answer.

Google's search results are based on highly sophisticated – and highly secret – sets of algorithms loosely based on whether Google 'likes' your website, and how your website relates to all the other large and small, and important and unimportant factors that make the worldwide web such an interesting and bewildering place.

In short – nobody's too sure. But what everyone *is* agreed on is that unless your site appears on page 1 of a Google search – and *maybe* page 2 – you might just as well not bother, because it'll never be visited.

If you've decided not to have a website, you can skim over the next few lines, because if you don't have a site – Google's not interested in you.

On the other hand, even if you've just gone down the route of using a site as a brochure, it'll get Google's wires humming...

This book isn't the place to start explaining the significance of Search Engine Optimisation; or keywords; or link-building; or the importance of headings.

They're really only of relevance if you decide to make your site your major business marketing tool, and you need to have either your site designer, or a specialist web optimisation person, go through the basics of this to you.

Be warned that it's not something that can be taken lightly, and when you're in – you're in. It's not an area you can try out for a while; decide it's too much effort; and stop. As I've mentioned previously, for a site to be successful for your business, it needs attention.

I spend about an hour online a day, every day, looking after the *Villasfor2* site. This will involve checking the daily results produced by Google's assorted analytical tools, which essentially tell me about,

- the various actions taken by visitors who logon to the *Villasfor2* site.

- tweaking any website pages that might need refreshing

- making sure the site works OK – so that when you click on something, you get taken to where you want to go,

- and finally, performing the same checks on our *mobile* site.

Because – yes – we have two sites. Why ? All sites are designed to be seen primarily on desktops or laptops. Seen on tablets or smartphones, because of the big differences in screen size, they don't fit so well. So, thanks to a little technological magic, we have a program that takes our 'main' site and scales it down to be legible and navigable on smaller devices.

If you're interested, take a look at the difference between *villasfor2.com*...and *m.villasfor2.com*

Web traffic on smartphones and tablets has been growing hugely, so having two versions of our site is good for us; and good for our position on key Google searches.

This, plus a raft of other factors means that *Villasfor2* appears on page 1 of Google searches that are of most importance to us – but it's a hard-won, and hard-maintained – achievement.

I did mention though that even if your website doesn't hold much more than some nice photos, and only gets updated when you've got a wet afternoon to fill, you can still take advantage of what Google can offer.

Locating your property on **Google Maps** and **Google Street View** is a lot of fun – and you can register yourself on **Google Business** too. It doesn't cost anything; is reasonably easy to figure-out; and most important of all, it does help to establish a little bit of online presence for you – and that's always a very good thing.

Social Networking

I'd be quite surprised if anyone reading this book hasn't got one – or both – of either a Facebook or Twitter personal account – and it's simple to extend your existing accounts to include your rentals business too.

With Twitter, you can open a new account in your business name. On

Facebook, you can add a business page to your personal page.

Why should you do this ? Aside from saying, 'because everyone else does it', the more reasoned arguments for establishing a social network presence for your business are because -

- it raises your business's profile

- it increases the number of hits on any website you might have

- it helps you to keep in contact and build relationships with past and future guests

- because Google's mysterious online search robots - or *searchbots* - like it !

In fact, Google will like it even more if you join their own social network platform G+...

It doesn't end there either. LinkedIn; Pinterest; Reddit – the list of social networking sites is well-nigh endless, so for reasons of time, practicality and common-sense, you have to decide early on how many of this type of site you can reasonably cope with - and draw a line under it.

Facebook and Twitter are givens. I'd personally add Pinterest – plus maybe one more from *either* LinkedIn. *Or* Reddit. *Or* G+.

But that said, social networking is constantly changing and evolving, and today's hot sites can be tomorrow's old news, so if you have friends or (young !) relatives who spend hours on line – ask them what's hot. And what's not...

Fitting Out Your Rental

As I mentioned several pages back, this particular section was going to be all about the tasks you'd be taking care of while your rental property was being prepared and made ready for guests. (I said you'd be busy...)

The good news is – you're nearly there ! On the other hand, you've still got one major hurdle ahead – and that's to go shopping for everything your guests are going to need during their stay with you.

Of course, what you're going to need – and how much of it you're going to need – is going to be entirely dependent on how you're going to be selling your rental, and the type of guests you're hoping to attract, so rather than get bogged-down in specific – and probably meaningless – detail, what I'm going to do is give you a series of checkpoints to think about; do something about; or decide they're not for you...

Your budget
Work out the absolute maximum amount you can spare for kitting-out your rentals. If you've got one unit – that's what you'll spend on it. If you have more than one unit, divide that number into the budget total to give you a cost-per-unit amount.

It's very important you do this *before* you've bought anything, because you're going to need *a lot* of stuff, and costs can very quickly spiral out of control unless you're working within strict confines.

TV – or no TV ? Satellite ? Cable ?
Villasfor2 is based in Italy and caters largely for British guests. Therefore having Italian TV - and the required licences - in each our rental units seems a pointless expense.

Satellite/cable channels offering English-language programmes can be very costly. We found that wiring-up our own home and our rental units – plus the resulting monthly subscription costs – would've been prohibitive.

Even just for a basic package – and human nature being what it is - it's odds-on our guests would've wondered why we didn't also have movies; and sport; and all the other optional extras...

That said, we actually *do* have TV sets in each of our villas – but they're just hooked-up to a DVD player. Over the years, we've built-up a big DVD library, which we top-up each year, (usually with the latest big

Oscar-winning movies).

It's a popular feature with our guests – and a good compromise to having no in-house entertainment at all.

Wireless internet access
An absolute , no-arguments, nailed-on necessity.

It's an undisputed feature of the way we live now that even on holiday, we like to have – *need* to have – all the necessary means to,

- keep in touch with friends and family

- to share our daily holiday experiences with them

- to access all the many and varied places on the internet that we're used to accessing

- and even to keep in touch with work.

We have a dedicated WLAN (Wireless Local Area Network) set up for our guests that was easy enough to establish from our own home broadband feed.

Bottom line is that (almost) regardless of cost, 24/7, on-demand internet access for your guests is a must – and you genuinely *do* run the risk of losing bookings – and getting negative reviews - if it's something you don't supply.

A washing machine (and tumble dryer ?)
We don't have a washing machine for our guests. In fact, because it never crossed our own minds to do anything more than maybe wash through a couple of odds-and-ends when we were away on holiday ourselves, we'd always assumed that everyone did what we did by going on holiday with a suitcase full of clean clothes – and going back home with a suitcase full of dirty ones.

In retrospect – possibly wrong...

However by the time we realised that perhaps a washing machine might have been useful, our preparations were so far advanced, there

114

was nowhere to actually put the thing.

So we compromised with bottles of hand-wash in each villa; plus a drying line, iron and ironing board available for communal use. Which, for the odd bits and pieces that some of our our guests do tend to wash out, has worked pretty well.

However...our guests are always adults – but if we catered for kids too, the picture would be very different.

Going purely by what we've been told from fellow-renters who *do* cater for family groups, kids on holiday do seem to get through *a lot* of clothes, and mums and dads appreciate the availability of a washing machine to take care of this.

Same applies for babies and toddlers – but perhaps more so !

So on the one hand, a washing machine is a useful and appreciated amenity for family groups – but perhaps not quite such a necessity for exclusively grown-up guests.

The downside though is that a washing machine can be an expensive luxury.

A family group, who are maybe used to doing a daily washing load at home won't think twice about doing the same when they're on holiday. After a day at the beach, a load of towels will be run through the wash too. Plus any bit of washing a guest fancies doing at any time – even if it's just a couple of items.

Not forgetting you'll be expected to supply detergent and fabric softener too, and because washing loads always seem to be done at peak electricity times during the day – the costs involved can be quite sharp. Even more so if you also supply a tumble dryer.

The washing machine/dryer question is an issue you'll need to address at the planning stage – and to be honest, there are so many pros and cons, I'm glad that for better/worse, it's a decision we've already made !

Furnishings. Fixtures. Fittings

If you're charging budget prices, you can supply budget facilities. Everything needn't necessarily be brand-new; or coordinate with everything else – and if you can save money by persuading friends and family to pass on unwanted items, then provided they're in decent condition and clean – that's fine.

On the other hand, the more you're charging, the higher your guests' expectations will (quite reasonably) be about what they'll find on their arrival.

Be very wary about describing either your rental – or what's inside – as 'luxury', because what *you* regard as luxurious, and what your guests regard as luxurious, could be miles apart. If you give your property a big build-up, and then fail to match your guests' expectations, you've immediately got a problem.

When we planning our own rentals venture, I asked for some advice about 'The Three Fs' from a friend who was running a holiday let in Portugal's Algarve.

That advice was simple: "Buy the best you can afford."

My friend explained the tried-and-tested reasoning behind this was that the better the quality of your furnishings, fixtures and fittings, the more likely they are to be respected by your guests.

And on the basis of our own experiences since 2009, I'd say that was unquestionably true.

Of course, accidents can – and do – happen when you're away on holiday just as easily as they can when you're at home, (especially when kids are added to the mix), so furniture that's well-made, sturdy, durable and – where necessary – with machine-washable covers, is a must.

And where's the best place to look for furnishing your rental ? If it's possible – IKEA.

Initially, we were dead against having our own Italian rentals looking like a Swedish furniture showroom, but regularly found that IKEA's combination of cost and quality was a far better bet than local alternatives.

In the end, we ended-up with a reasonable mix-and-match Italian/Swedish compromise – though our determination to buy Italian wherever we could wasn't always easy. Like a bed arriving with four different-size legs...

What you'll actually need will be governed by how many people will be staying in your property, but speaking generally, each of your guests will need somewhere...

- to sleep

- to sit and relax

- to sit and eat

- to prepare food

- to wash

So each of your rentals must have as a minimum:

- bedroom(s) – or designated sleeping area(s), with bedside tables and lights; and wardrobe with hangers and drawers for clothes. While you may go for fixed double beds as your 'default', don't lose sight of the need for single beds too.

- There must of course be sleeping space – either a double bed, or a single - available for each guest.

    If you don't have sufficient bedrooms/sleeping areas to accommodate the required number of beds without overcrowding or compromising privacy, you'll need to think of sofa-beds – or something similar.

    If that's not possible, you have no alternative but to reduce your maximum capacity.

- Best option if you can find them are doubles with 'ziplock' mattresses that can quickly be converted into singles. (This kind of bed is unknown in Italy – so we ended fixing-up our own. Which was surprisingly easy to do...)

- If space allows, a dressing table and chair are a useful optional extra.

- If you're catering for kids, you'll need bunk and/or single beds – and cots/buggy space for babies and toddlers.

- a sitting room – or designated area with sofas, easy chairs, maybe a coffee table. You may decide to install a sofa bed here.

  We've already discussed the pros and cons of having a TV set, or just - as we do - a TV and DVD player.

  You may want to add an audio system; or iPod/MP3 docking station; or games consoles.

- an eating area – which can be in the kitchen; or sitting room; or even a separate dining room. A dining table should ideally be large enough for as many people as possible - in relation to the rental's size - to sit, eat, drink and socialise together.

  If you're catering for very young children, you will need high-chair(s).

- a kitchen – or designated area with a free-standing cooker (or fitted 4-burner hob and separate oven/grill); refrigerator; sink /drainer. Plus storage sufficient for cooking utensils, crockery and cutlery, and non-perishable food.

  Should you choose, a kitchen lends itself to a variety of optional extras: microwave; freezer; dishwasher; coffee-maker; electric kettle; toaster; food processor/smoothie-maker.

- A bathroom/shower room, with bath and/or shower; toilet; sink; towel rails; shaving mirror; hairdryer/shaver sockets;

storage for shampoo and assorted personal hygiene products.

A bidet is a good optional extra – or even supplied as standard.

If you're accepting very young children, your bathroom should have adequate space for nappy-changing – and you'll need to provide nappy-disposal facilities too. Also remember that if you just fit-out a shower-room, you may need to talk to parents about the need for a baby-bath.

Throughout your rental, you'll need adequate power points to recharge computers, phones, electric toothbrushes, cameras – and all the other devices that guests arrive with !

Crockery. Cutlery. Glassware. Utensils. Towels. Bedding and Linen

This is where we start talking numbers that might make your eyes pop a little...

The easy bit first...
As regards crockery, cutlery and kitchen utensils – take a look at the sample inventory a little further on to get an idea of what you need to supply in each rental unit you have – and how many of each item.

As regards crockery, cutlery and glassware there are two key guidelines to give you:

- go for exactly the same style and colour of crockery/cutlery in each of the rental units you have – and the same styles of glassware. This makes replacing breakages so much easier. Wherever you can, it's much cheaper to buy sets of crockery/cutlery/glasses, rather than individual pieces.

- buy whatever you think you're going to need to start you off – and then buy one complete extra set of crockery, cutlery - and two extra sets of each type of glass. These will be your spares to use when items get broken.

Kitchen utensils – the pots, pans - and all the other odds-and-ends that you'll always find in kitchen drawers - don't need replacing that often, so there's no real need to keep spares in stock. Just get new ones on an 'as-needed' basis.

When it comes to towels, bedding and linen...

- once again, for reasons of being able to use *all* your towels and linen in *all* your rental units - and for ease of replacement - go for exactly the same style and colour across the board.

- choice of colour is up to you. We went for white both for bedlinen and towels, which is safe and always looks good. Only downside to white is that sunscreen stains – especially the types that also include a bronzer – can be incredibly difficult to remove from towels.

  Which is why you'll also need colourful pool/patio/beach towels, which don't mark-up so obviously !

- we've found that as far as bedlinen is concerned, polycotton is a better bet than pure cotton. Main reason for this is that polycotton doesn't need ironing - and ironing sheets is something that only a commercial laundry can reliably do well.

  And if you have your bedlinen washed commercially – it'll add to your costs. Polycotton is also harder-wearing than pure cotton.

- on your beds, duvets are all-round winners compared to blankets. Go for the 'all-season' type, which provides two duvets in the same pack – a lightweight one for summer; mid-weight for spring and autumn; and joined together for winter.

  Buy one extra double and single duvet set to cover for emergencies.

As regards the exact numbers of everything you're going to need:

- work out the number of individual towels and items of bedlinen you'd need if your rental(s) was occupied to maximum capacity.

- multiply those numbers by three to discover the overall total number you'll need to buy.

How does that work ? You need operate on the principle of, 'one in use; one in the wash; one spare.'

Preparing a double bed for the arrival of guests, you'd need:

- 1 x under-sheet

- 1 x duvet cover

- 4 x pillow cases

So you'd actually need to buy:

- 3 x under-sheets

- 3 x duvet covers

- 12 x pillow cases

Follow that formula for all the beds you have in your property and make similar calculations for single beds, cots, and/or bunk beds too. If you intend supplying mattress protectors, or any other items of bedding, follow the same formula to work out how many to buy.

For a bathroom, per guest you might supply:

- 1 x small towel

- 1 x medium towel

- 1 x large towel

- 1 x pool/beach towel

So you'd need to buy:

- 3 x small towels

- 3 x medium towels

- 3 x large towels
- 3 x pool/bath towels

...and then in turn multiply *those* totals by the maximum number of guests you can accommodate.

Don't forget other items of linen like bathmats, tea-towels, etc if you intend supplying any of these.

The large numbers of everything now in front of you may seem excessive - but they'll be a safeguard against running out of spares at the times you need them. (And there *will* be times like these...)

And even if you *do* find you've over-bought, it'll mean you can rotate all your items through all rental periods, which in turn will mean they'll last longer and so reduce the need for replacements.

Incidentally, in case you're wondering how often you should supply your guests with a change of towels and bedlinen, we operate on the principle of providing a full change midway through any stay of longer than 7 nights.

Where to buy ? And how to keep clean ?

You might also ask how best to get hold of the large quantities of towels and linen you're going to need. The answer we found was to buy good quality hotel-standard items from commercial suppliers. This was substantially cheaper than buying the same quantity we needed from retail outlets, and we found the quality extremely good.

We obtained quotes from a couple of suppliers we found online, and both were happy to send us samples to help us make our choice. As it turned out, the most expensive part of all this was having all this shipped put from the UK to Italy. (Big bundles of towels and linen weigh *a lot* !)

with the benefit of hindsight, it would've been even better to buy what we needed before we left the UK and then added everything to our house-move.

You'll also need to think about the large amounts of washing you'll need to cope with as each group of guests leaves your property. Doing it yourself is – as discussed – the cheapest option. Aim to get hold of a large-capacity washer from a good manufacturer.

This really is one area where the budget option just won't pay-off, as you'll be making your washing machine work hard.

And give a thought to where you'll dry washing. Outside is easy enough in summer – and there's something special about sun-dried sheets and towels.

But if possible, try not to have loads of washing hanging out to dry on the days guests arrive, as it doesn't make for the best of first impressions...

Outside

Regardless whether there's just one communal outdoor area – or whether each rental unit has its own private outdoor space - you'll need plenty of weatherproof furniture. Enough tables/chairs for all your guests is a prerequisite – and should be easy to meet, as the choice and price range of patio furniture is enormous. If you feel you can run to sun umbrellas and sunbeds too – great !

Personally, I'd avoid anything made of moulded plastic, because it just has a low-end feel (and doesn't last that long either).

If you have the outdoor space, a barbecue is always a big favourite, though with the kind of use it's likely to get, you're better off with one of the large capacity, gas-fuelled variety. Charcoal may be cheaper – but it'll be you cleaning it out after every use and topping-up supplies every day.

The Inventory

If you set about it methodically, fitting-out your rentals is actually quite straightforward.

Just think what *you'd* need for a week's stay – and start from there !

But if you'd like a little guidance in getting your shopping list together, here's the complete inventory of how our own villas are fitted out.

Feel free to copy it or adapt it however you want for your own rentals...

<u>Furniture</u>

- Refrigerator
- Dining table
- Two dining chairs

- Sofa
- Coffee table
- Armchair
- Bookcase

- Wardrobe
- Radiator
- AC unit + remote control

- Chest of drawers
- Double bed and double mattress
- (or two single beds + mattresses)
- Two bedside tables
- Wicker chair

You have considerable room for manoeuvre as regards furniture styles and quality, though n.b. the point that the better the quality, the more consideration will be shown by guests.

That said, there are limits. Unless you intend having a restricted and high-end clientele, it's simple

common sense not to equip a rental with antiques or expensive designer furniture. The watchwords should

always be comfort, durability – and easy to clean !

If you have more than one rental unit, consider fitting them out identically, so that none is 'better' than the

others. It also makes swapping-round replacement items so much easier.

Ensure you've always got a good supply of replacement lightbulbs in stock !

Contents – (Based on a couple sharing)

Towels and Linen

- 2 white bidet towels
- 2 white hand towels
- 4 white bath towels
- 1 white bathmat
- 2 coloured pool towels (velour)
- 2 coloured beach towels (terry)
- 4 white pillowcases
- 1 white under-sheet
- 1 white over-sheet
- 1 mattress protector
- 1 floral-pattern bed cover
- 1 white duvet cover
- 1 double duvet
- 4 pillows

Sleeping Area

- 2 wall mirrors
- 2 pictures
- Personal safe
- 2 bedside lights

- Small waste-bin
- Red/white cushion

Bathroom

- Hairdryer
- Soap dispenser
- Shower soap holder
- Small pedal bin
- Toilet brush
- Shower tidy
- Mirror and shelf unit

Living Area

- TV + remote control
- DVD player + remote control
- Round glass table lamp
- Standard lamp
- Cushion
- Umbrella
- Doormat
- Window curtain
- Various pictures, photographs and ornaments.

Kitchen

- Kitchen towel holder
- Block of 4 kitchen knives
- Wood chopping board
- Paper napkin holder
- Coffee maker
- Kettle
- Olive oil bottle
- Plate drying rack; tea towel
- Pair oven mitts
- Lighter
- Box of sticking plasters
- Torch

- Scissors
- Dustpan & brush
- Large terracotta bowl

Utensils

- 4 knives; 4 forks
- 4 dessert spoons; 4 teaspoons
- Plastic colander
- Terracotta utensils holder

- Plastic spatula; straining spoon
- Plastic pasta scoop; serving spoon
- Potato peeler; wooden spoons; grater

- Garlic press; can opener
- S/M/L saucepans; Pasta pot
- Frying pan
- Lever corkscrew
- Stainless steel bowl

Glass & Crockery

- 1 litre glass carafe

- 4 wine glasses
- 4 tumblers
- 2 white mugs
- 2 coloured coffee cups
- 4 white side-plates
- 2 white dinner plates
- 4 large white bowls
- 2 plastic 'pool glasses'

Sun Terrace

- Round wooden table

- 2 folding wooden chairs + cushions

- Wooden sun umbrella

- Terracotta umbrella base

Particularly as regards crockery and glassware, you'll have bought sufficient stocks to allow for breakages –

and you'll have also worked out how much you'll need in the way of towels and bedlinen to allow for the formula of, 'one in use; one in the wash; one spare'.

We've also quipped our own rentals with non-stick pots and pans – hence our use of plastic utensils to keep them from getting scratched !

Basic Supplies

In addition to the furnishing, fixtures and fittings, it'll be up to you what you supply in the way of basics so your guests won't need to rush off to the shops the minute they arrive.

Holiday rentals are essentially self-catering, but many owners supply a 'welcome pack' with a few essentials like tea and coffee. From our own experience, guests also welcome the provision of items like sugar, salt and pepper on the basis that if they have to buy these on arrival, pack sizes are far bigger than they'll realistically need during their stay with you.

At the very least, your guests should find...

- Toilet paper and spare rolls

- Bathroom soap

- Washing-up liquid

- Sponge and scourer for washing-up

- Garbage bags

- Hand-wash detergent

- Sugar, salt and pepper

When – during our own setting-up process – we were checking-out to see what other rental owners offered in the way of 'standard supplies', we were astonished to discover how little was generally laid-on for guests.

In one case – not even toilet paper...

It costs very little to appear lavish in the way of what your guests will find waiting for them – and it really does get noticed and appreciated.

The Last Thing To Do Before You Open

Test everything out !

Really ?

Absolutely ! And I don't mean just flicking the lights on and off and flushing the toilet. (Though you'll be checking this is all OK too).

Basic question is how are you going to be 100% sure that everything in your rental is just as it should be unless you spend a couple of days staying there yourself ?

And if you have more than one rental unit, it really is a case of spending a little time in *all* of them.

You need to put yourself in the position of someone staying on holiday in your rental and ensuring not only that everything works properly, but that,

- the beds are comfortable

- the water in the kitchen and bathroom is hot and plentiful

- the internet connection is fast

- the heating and/or air-conditioning are working

- you haven't skimped in your supply of anything from crockery and cutlery to towels and bedding

- everything is fresh and squeaky-clean.

Make sure you know how any electrical equipment – like an air-con unit, a DVD player or a microwave – all works, so you can confidently explain this to your guests, rather than going off to find a manual.

If something's wrong, how many million times better is it to get it fixed *before* your guests arrive, rather than *after* ?

(And yes – we *did* find a couple of little glitches when we road-tested our own rentals before we opened...)

4. RUNNING YOUR BUSINESS

The planning and the setting-up are over. Your new holiday rentals business is up-and-running. You're starting to take bookings – and make some money ! And I very much hope you'll now be thinking doing this was quite a good idea after all !

Now you've got to build on all the hard work you've put in to start your business. You need to establish a way of working that suits you/your partner/the family members who are involved with you – *and* which enables you to actually enjoy what you're doing. (Well...most of the time anyway...)

This will include...

- Who does what ? (And taking a bit of time off...)

- Handling your bookings.

- Tax and insurance

- Getting on with guests

- The importance of good reviews

- ...and how to deal with bad ones..

- Looking after your property

"But I thought *you* were looking after this..."

No matter how carefully you've thought ahead, once you've started for real, things have a habit of taking on a life of their own and you'll need to make little adjustments to any previous ideas and plans you might have made.

At this early stage, the worst thing you can do is start off with a rigid outlook as to how your business *should* operate, and try and make what *is* happening fit in with your ideas about what *ought* to be

133

happening.

Far better to adapt your plans and your way of working to the reality of how your business is unfolding and settling down.

For your rentals business to work well, everyone involved needs to be absolutely clear of their own responsibilities. If this happens, it minimises the chances of something being missed because A thought B was going to do it – and B thought A was...

At the start of this book, I explained that in our case, Pauline takes care of every aspect of what goes on *inside* our rental villas (and our own home); and I look after what happens *outside*.

It's a division of work and responsibilities that's worked well for us both for so long now, that what we need to do, and when and how we need to do it - fitted around the comings and goings of our rental guests - is almost second nature.

The knock-on effect of this experience is that because we now have a pretty good idea how long each of the individual tasks in our respective domains is likely to take, we can fix our own schedule to take care of it. Not only is that a nice thing to be able to do, it also makes it easier to help-out if either of us needs a hand with anything, or if something unexpected crops up.

In developing a schedule that suits you best, you'll discover there'll be days when you're very busy. Days when you're not so busy. And days when you find you have nothing much to do at all.

And the nature of the holiday rentals business being what it is, those days won't obligingly always fall at the same time each week, but will rather be scattered at random across your calendar.

So while you'll quickly realise that running a rental most definitely isn't a Monday-Friday, 9-5 job, If your rental is seasonal it won't be a 24/7/365 effort either.

Much as you might hope to be busy throughout the year, if your rental is primarily a summer one, there'll be periods off-season when your time will be exclusively yours.

This is when we do any necessary maintenance jobs that can't be fitted-in when we're busy - but it's also a time to relax, not do very much, and recharge our batteries.

The only exception to this might be if you have a rental that *is* in use throughout the year - a city-based one perhaps. While looking after this type of rental is outside my own experience, the principle of balancing work/downtime would still apply – even more so - though it may be harder to achieve.

As we've found in our own situation, even at our busiest periods of the year, our respective responsibilities give each of us a bit of personal free time while the other might be busy – and regular time together too. That's important, even if it involves not a lot more than going our for a meal or a drink; seeing friends; or taking in one of our local fairs and festivals.

At quieter times of the year, you'll find you're able to take holidays of your own, or get to know your new country better, because there's not much point relocating from one country to another - and then only seeing the bit of it you own !

Taking Care Of Bookings

Research carried out by the big lettings agencies has shown that once a prospective guest has decided to book a holiday at your rental, they want that booking process to be as quick and easy as possible. At worst – something that can be wrapped-up inside a day. At best – inside an hour.

There's no room for errors. The way you handle your bookings has got to be fast and flawless. Each time. Every time. Consequently, based on my own experience, I really do recommend just one person takes care of this.

Why ? Because while I know and accept that many rentals divide up the assorted aspects of the bookings process, I just feel mistakes are less likely to be made if only one of you handles everything.

As you're about to discover, broken down into into their individual components, the list of all the factors involved in each booking seems a long and challenging one – (though each component part isn't in itself especially difficult) - so it's *much* easier for just one person to evolve and become familiar with their own particular way of keeping track of all this, rather than two people...or even more...

Dealing with enquiries – and accepting a booking

If an enquiry has been triggered from your own website, the first you'll know about it will be either by email or phone.

(Assuming – hopefully – your website has a Contacts Form (which I touched-on in the previous section)...and also lists your phone number. (Which – remember – will be a dedicated, business-only cellphone, which you'll always have with you).

If the enquiry's come from a rentals listings agency, chances are you'll get both an email *and* an sms text message to your business cellphone. Most agencies use this twin-alert system.

There aren't many enquiry variants: someone either wants to make a booking, but needs your confirmation their chosen dates are free. Or find out what it'd cost to stay with you between date A and date B.

You'll also get the occasional enquiry asking about your 'best price' for a holiday – a polite way of discovering if you give discounts. (And whether you do or not - and how much - is entirely up to you !)

Time is now of the essence and you need to reply to your enquiry within 30 minutes at the outside. If your prospective guest has supplied a phone number with their enquiry – give them a ring. Not only does this provide an excellent first impression of your speed and efficiency, but it also probably puts you at the head of the queue if the person asking about a booking with you has also made similar enquiries to other rentals.

(If they ask about your 'best price', while they can - as I mention above - be trying to see how much money off you're prepared to give them, they can also be trawling the rental market for the best deal !)

If there's no phone number, still stick to that 30 minute benchmark for replying to that initial enquiry with an email reply.

Listings agencies don't pass on phone numbers – or email addresses either. All contact with a prospective guest is initially done through them. (Otherwise it'd be too easy for you to bypass them; deal with an enquirer yourself; and save on any bookings commission !)

As regards how quickly you reply to enquiries, listings agencies use your enquiry response time as one of the factors they employ to determine where you appear on their listings – so that gives you even more of an incentive to reply quickly.

You may exchange a number of mails – or phone calls – with a possible guest over a fairly short period of time until a moment when – Yes ! They'd like to go ahead and book; or, No ! Sorry...not this time.

I wish there was some sort of formula that could be applied to get the percentage of enquiries that turn into firmed-up bookings...

There isn't – or at least, not one that I've managed to discover...

Sometimes you'll get an idea about why you've missed out. Aside from something obvious like not having the right dates available, maybe you're a bit too expensive; or the flights and car rental costs bump up the price too much. Or maybe how you've configured your rental isn't quite right. Or maybe the local shops aren't close enough.

Most of the time though, you probably won't have a clue why you've missed out.

For every reason to choose a holiday destination – there's also a reason not to choose it. If you've lost out on a booking because of some easily-fixable reason – then fix it.

Otherwise, try not to take it personally – and look forward to the next enquiry !

Flexibility

When we started, we had the idea that all bookings would conveniently run from Saturday-Saturday.

It didn't take very long to realise this wasn't a very good idea, or a very practical one...

- It made no allowance for guests who wanted to take advantage of lower weekday air fares and book a week-long stay from – say – Monday – Monday...

- ...or guests who might be quite happy to arrive on a Saturday - but then wanted to stay for 10 nights and leave on a Tuesday.

- And what about guests who just wanted a short break ? Could they arrive on a Friday for a long weekend and go home on the Monday ?

Our policy needed a rapid rethink...

Unless at a quiet time of the year, we only have a major problem with a 7 night booking running Wednesday-Wednesday, (on the basis that it leaves an unrentable gap at the start of the first week...and at the end of the second week).

We generally find we can work round 7-night bookings starting/ending on other midweek nights.

Bookings of between 8 and 13 nights starting/ending on any day of the week are actually much easier to fit in. Yes, they too leave gaps at the start and and end of weeks – but these gaps can be of 4, 5 or 6 nights, which allows us to sell them off as cut-price 'bargain breaks'.

Bookable short breaks – as opposed to gap-filling set dates - can be a major revenue earner, especially if available flights make long weekends a possibility.

On the other hand, you may also want to think about a 'minimum stay' requirement on your rental on the basis of the time and effort it takes you to prepare for a very short stay – and the (relatively low) revenue you earn from it.

We set minimum stay requirements throughout the year: It's 3 nights - except for late June-early September, when it's 7.

Having flexibility in your bookings requirements will certainly increase your revenue – and it also illustrates an important factor in any holiday rentals business:

The best and most successful ones work around the requirements of their guests. Not their owners,

"Can you hold these dates for me ?"
This isn't an unusual request – but it can be a problem !

On the face of it – it seems a perfectly reasonable request. A prospective guest first wants to confirm with you whether their preferred dates are free. If they are, can you please hold them while they arrange to take time off work/book flights/etc ?

That's generally OK if you have multiple rental units free for the dates in question, and/or the prospective booking is for a quiet time of year. It's *not* OK if you only have one free unit, and/or the booking's for the middle of summer !

My response is always the same –

"Yes, I'll be happy to hold these dates for you until you've made your arrangements. If in the meantime someone else also wants those dates, I'll ring you immediately and ask you to firm-up your booking right away. If you're not able to do that, I'm afraid I'll have to take the new offer instead of yours."

This seems a fair and reasonable compromise – and one that to date has always been accepted by prospective guests.

One thing I *won't* ever do however is mark-off our availability calendar as 'provisionally booked', because if it gets to be seen that you're OK with accepting provisional bookings, they'll soon take over your calendar – and you'll run the risk of losing 'real' bookings as a result.

Dates are either 'booked' – or 'available' !

Your Availability Calendar
Time to revisit this no-cost/low-cost essential !

When an enquiry turns into a booking, it's down to you to ensure it's handled professionally and properly.

First, double-check the chosen dates are free on your availability calendar.

If you don't have one primary calendar that's your first port of call for checking dates, you'll be running the risk of making some career-threatening mistakes. And even if you *do* faithfully record all your bookings on that primary calendar, you'll also find you're going to be using more than just one...

- I have a calendar hanging up next to the phone in my office so if anyone calls, I can instantly see which dates are free – and which aren't. That's my shared primary reference.

- I have another on my cellphone, so if I get an enquiry when I'm away from home, I have the necessary details on hand. That's my other shared primary reference !

- Yes – of course ! - I have one on the *Villasfor2* website, but that's really so site visitors can see if we have availability when they're thinking of taking a holiday.

- And there are calendars too on each of the rentals agencies where we're listed.

That all makes for quite a few calendars – and whenever you take a new booking, it has to be recorded on each of them as soon as possible.

Don't panic ! This is nowhere near as complicated or time-consuming as it looks !

No getting away from the fact that the paper calendar on my wall needs filling-in by hand. (Not a problem that arises if you steer away from pen-and-paper !)

However rentals agency calendars can now be automatically synchronised across a wide range of your online devices, and if you choose your own cellphone/website programs carefully, just one entry will be all you ever need to keep all your availability calendars everywhere fully updated.

One of the biggest sins in the holiday rentals business is not keeping your calendar up-to-date. Because nothing is guaranteed to irritate a potential guest more than to discover that dates that *appear* free on your calendar, in fact aren't free at all.

Because you've forgotten to mark a previously-made booking as 'Unavailable'.

The initial reaction from your potential guest will usually be to go and look for a rental somewhere else which is genuinely free for their chosen dates, rather than wait to hear from you when you can fit them in.

Can you really blame them ? Especially if they've already made preliminary arrangements to take the necessary time off work; checked out flight and car rental prices around their preferred dates – and liaised with any friends who might be part of their booking.

Not unreasonably they might be disinclined to do this all over again.

I won't go into the scenario where you've agreed dates and prices for a booking with a potential guest; taken money from them; forgotten to mark-up the booking on your calendar – and then taken a subsequent booking from another guest for the same dates...

The dreaded double-booking. It happens. But happily, never to us – and hopefully never to you either.

Not surprisingly then – in view of how important it is - keeping your calendar up-to-date and accurate is another parameter which listings agencies use to rank where you're listed.

The Payment Process

Depending on the time gap between a booking being confirmed, and the arrival date, you'll be asking a guest either for a reservation deposit – or full payment.

To give you an idea, we work around a cut-off point of 6 weeks. Any guest booking a stay with us *more* than 6 weeks before their arrival date would be asked for a deposit of €150; any booking made *less* than 6 weeks before arrival date would be asked for immediate payment in full. A guest who'd previously paid a deposit would then be asked for the balance payment at the 6 week point.

I know that many rental owners prefer to charge a percentage amount of a total holiday cost – usually 20-25% - as a reservation deposit. We charge a flat rate, regardless of the length of stay, as we simply find it easier. Either is perfectly fine – and it's entirely your call.

Some owners also regard reservation deposits as non-refundable in the event of a subsequent cancellation. While I'd never argue with an owner's right to run their rental entirely as they see fit, as a holidaymaker, I'd personally never book anywhere with this policy in force, as it just seems one-sided and unduly punitive.

When we need to deal with a cancellation – which in fact doesn't happen that often – we retain a token sum from a deposit to cover the costs we incur in making a refund. Nobody ever cancels a holiday lightly and it just seems wrong to harshly penalise someone when this happens.

I understand the reasoning behind non-refundable deposits – it gives an owner some financial protection against not being able to re-let the gap on their calendar left by a cancellation, and it also discourages time-wasters. But it's just not for us – and once again, it's your call about what you'll do in these situations.

The Security Deposit

There is however one form of deposit you'll always be delighted to return in full – and that's the security – or breakage - deposit.

This is a sum of money, added to your guest's final payment, which will be used to pay for any damage and/or breakages they cause while staying with you. Some owners also use this type of deposit to pay for any extra cleaning that might be deemed necessary after a guest leaves.

How much should a security/breakage deposit be ? We charge €100, but know that some owners – especially those who cater for kids – charge €200-€300.

Generally, we're reasonably relaxed about what – if anything – we take from a security deposit. On the basis that accidents can happen, we don't deduct anything if the odd glass or item of crockery gets damaged/broken during a guest's stay.

Similarly, we won't make any charge if anything's broken/damaged that doesn't cost much to replace, or can be repaired.

We've always found the vast majority of our own guests respect our rental villas, and what's inside them – and in return we won't deduct anything from a security deposit unless we genuinely feel there's no alternative.

Consequently, in the ten-odd years we've been in business at the time of writing this book, I don't think I've made more than four or five charges against deposits.

In just one of those cases was it necessary to withhold the entire security deposit amount.

There have also been just a couple of occasions when guests have accidentally caused damage costing more than €100 to set right, but in both those cases, our guests accepted responsibility for the mishap and made the necessary covering payment.

Returning a security deposit is simple. If a guest has added this to a PayPal or rentals agency payment, it's a quick and easy online transaction, and something we always aim to do within 24 hours of a guest leaving.

Some owners collect a deposit in cash from their guests on arrivals, and return it the day they leave. However as this involves checking through your rental while your guests are hanging around wanting to do nothing more than head off to the airport, it's not an especially satisfactory thing to do – and not something I'd recommend.

However I do strongly recommend preparing a full inventory of furnishings and contents – like those I showed you a short while ago - and making two copies before each arrival. Sign both copies yourself confirming everything's in good order – and ask your guests to do likewise. They keep one copy – you keep the other.

Should any mishap then occur, there can be no argument that 'it was like that when we got here.'

Collecting your guests' details
After you've dealt with the enquiry; agreed a price – and the dates – for a stay at your rental; blocked-off the relevant period on your availability calendar; and taken some money. What next ?

Well...you'll need to have all the details of the booking in one place, so you can refer to it quickly, and you can do this either on your computer, or the old-fashioned, low-tech way on paper.

(Which – out of pure personal preference – is what we do).

What are the details we need ? Here's the information that goes on our own 'Guest Details' form, and it's what we've found we need to ensure that all aspects of any particular booking are covered.

Use this as a template and adapt it however suits you best...

- As we have three rental villas, the first thing that goes on our Guest Details form is which of those three is being booked – plus our guests' arrival and departure dates.

- The number of guests.

Doesn't really apply to us, as we only ever have two in each of our rentals ! But it might well be something you need to know...

- The names of guests.
  In our case, we take the names of both people staying. It'll take a bit more effort for you to collect the names of everyone included in a larger group, but it's something that needs to be done so you can sort out the sleeping arrangements. (See immediately below). When taking a booking for a larger group, establish as early as you can the name of the 'main guest' who'll be your primary contact for all aspects of the booking and payment.

- Guest set-up
  When a booking's being made for a group of people, you'll need to know who's partnering who, so you can set-up the necessary sleeping arrangements. And if any kids are included in the booking, you'll need to know their ages - so you can make the appropriate sleeping arrangements for them too ! - and also whether or not they'll be sharing a room with other family members.

- The address of your main guest.

- A phone number for your main guest.
  Ideally, both a landline and a cellphone number. It'll be cheaper for you to call a landline before your guests arrive. You'll need a cellphone number in case you need to call them for any reason while they're actually staying with you.

- An email address for your main guest.

- The source of the booking.
  For your own records, you might find it useful to know whether the booking originated from your own website – or from whichever of the rentals agencies you might be listed

with.

- The booking date.
  (When the actual booking was made)

- The number of nights your guests are staying.

- The agreed cost of your guests' stay.

- Security/breakage deposit.
  If you're charging one – you'll need to make a note of it – and whether any you've made any subsequent deductions.

- The payment method.
  Paypal ? Through one of your listings agencies ? Some other method ?

- If a booking deposit payment is being taken, the amount of money involved; the date it was paid; and the date it was returned – with a note of any deductions made for breakages/damage.

- Payment notes.
  Details of any commission payments to be deducted, and/or any other relevant information about how guests are paying for their stay,

- Balance A.
  This will be the agreed cost of the booking *minus* any booking deposit you've already taken and *minus* any commissions paid out.

- Balance B.
  This will be the relevant amount in Balance A, *plus* what you charge for any security/breakage deposit. This will be full and final amount your guest will pay for their holiday.

- Final payment date.
  When you've taken a booking deposit, the date when Balance

146

B – the full and final holiday payment - is due. Also note here if a guest will need a little email/phone heads-up from you shortly before this final payment is due.

If the booking's been made within 6 weeks of arrival, and you've asked for immediate full payment of the cost involved, you'll have previously decided your policy about the timeframe within which this payment should be made. Bearing in mind that as payments using PayPal – or a rentals agency payment system – are virtually instantaneous, allowing 48 hours for your guest to complete the transaction isn't unreasonable.

- Final payment received.
  The date you receive the money.

- Availability Calendar.
  Tick that you've marked-off the dates of the booking on *each* of yours !

- Cash book.
  More about this in a moment... Basically, you'll need to keep financial records of your business, and a cash book – or something similar – is where you'll do it. Tick that you've recorded the financial details of this particular booking

- Arrival airport and/or other travel details.
  How a guest intends to reach you ! Also a good idea to note flight arrival times, so you have a rough idea when your guests will be turning up.

- Guest Info.
  Once a guest has paid their final balance, we email them an Info Pack, which includes directions from their arrival airport; details of what they'll find when they arrive here – and more ! At the very least, you'll need to send directions and/or satnav details.

- Notes.

Any other info/reminders you need regarding this booking.

As I said a short while ago, while the bookings procedure must right now be seeming an alarming prospect – it really isn't. And it won't take long before you're rattling through it each time you take a booking.

However, as I hope I've shown, it really does have to be a job for just one person to develop on their own, rather than attempt to share it out.

Your Financial Responsibilities

It's a sad, but unavoidable, fact that once you've set-up your rentals business and are earning money from it, at some point you're probably going to have to pay some tax.

The sensible plan is to work out the best possible tax regimen for your business and other assorted personal circumstances before you start trading, and line-up a good local accountant who can look after any day-to-day issues that arise once you've started.

At the very least, you'll need to keep accurate financial records about your business, because it's from these that your accountant will prepare your annual tax returns and calculate what tax payments you'll need to make.

In order to do this, your accountant should explain to you in detail the exact financial information they'll need. Your responsibility is then to ensure you have it.

Insurance and Liabilities

At the home you lived in before embarking on your new venture, you'll probably have had insurance to cover both the building itself; and the fixtures, fittings, furnishings and personal possessions inside.

You may want to do exactly the same for your new home – and add cover for your rentals, and what's inside them.

In any event however, you need to give serious consideration to Liability Insurance. If you're not sure what that actually is, it's basically insurance cover for you if you get a claim for damages from any guest who has allegedly suffered an accident, injury or loss while staying at your property.

Good liability cover will provide you with legal representation in this kind of situation, and meet the cost of any damages award made against you – which in serious cases can be incredibly high.

We have substantial liability cover bundled-up with our own regular house/contents insurance. In this day and age it seems an absolute necessity.

Many owners think likewise. Some, citing the cost of this type of insurance cover, don't. Personally, for the peace of mind it provides, (and the not excessively high premiums involved), I think liability cover is money well-spent.

Getting On With Guests

When it comes to dealing with guests in the early days of running your holiday rentals business, you'll find it's a bit of a balancing act between being easily available whenever a guest wants you for anything – but not so much as to start being an intrusive nuisance...

As we've discovered, guests don't really want to be constantly asked if everything's OK, or if they need anything; but they *do* like you to be around when they want to ask directions; book a restaurant; borrow a guidebook; or simply have a chat.

If – like us – you live on the same bit of land where your rentals are situated, the very fact you'll visibly be around taking care of the day-to-day running of your business will be reassuring if anyone wants you for anything. While you might also let your guests know – as we do – they're always welcome to come to our house if they need us.

On that latter point, you perhaps need to be a little more careful than we originally were. We genuinely don't mind when a guest comes knocking at the door. But it does wear a little thin sometimes when this happens early; or late; or right in the middle of lunch !

You might like to consider – as in retrospect, we might've done – putting a note on your door that tells guests you'll always be happy to see them between - say - 0900–1300...and 1500-1900, to keep their visits within reasonable limits.

Over the years, we've developed a routine whereby one of us is always around to greet our guests on their arrival; show them to their villa and check them in; explain how everything works; and answer any initial questions they have.

We'll then see them again at some point during the following day, to make sure they've settled-in and have everything they need.

After that, a guest needn't necessarily have any contact with us at all until they leave at the end of their holiday. Or we might see them for something every day.

Either – and anything in-between - is just fine and entirely their call and - going by the comments some have made when reviewing their holidays here - they appreciate the fact we always seem to be around when we're needed, but melt into the background when we're not.

It's a useful knack to have !

Dealing with disputes
Even the best-run business can sometimes hit a problem. How you deal with it will be the difference between it being just a minor glitch – or becoming a major issue.

You'll have heard of that old saying, "The customer is always right" You know what ? It's true !

Never argue. Never become confrontational. Never be aggressive.

Always listen. Always apologise. Always be polite.

Winning an argument, or proving a point in the event of a mishap may make you feel better – but it'll make your guest feel worse, and in the long run, that'll only rebound on you in the form of a bad review, or adverse comments to their friends and family.

Even if you're absolutely, unquestionably 100% in the right on the issue in question and it *seriously* annoys you to acknowledge otherwise – still politely defer to your guest, however unpleasantly or unreasonably they might be acting. (And however unpleasant and unreasonable this might seem to you).

Bottom line is this: in a week or so, they'll be going home and you'll never see them again. And you have their money. Hold that thought...

Being understanding, apologetic, and unfailingly polite – perhaps backing this up with a nice bottle of wine - will defuse 99% of all potentially awkward situations. For the rare – *very* rare – occasions that escalate, the surrounding circumstances will dictate how you react. There are no hard-and-fast rules. But as long as you remain calm and in control it should ensure that emotions are kept within bounds, with– hopefully – common-sense and compromise winning out.

House Rules
We're not talking here about a forbidding set of Do's and Don'ts nailed to your rental property's door. We *are* however talking about a few guidelines you'll want your guests to observe when they're staying with you.

We have one:

- No Smoking. Anywhere. Inside or outside.

Inside ? Understandable. But outside too ? That's easily explained. If you're relaxing on a sunbed alongside our pool, you don't want to catch wafts of cigarette smoke on the breeze. Same applies when you're sitting outside your villa having a nice glass of wine as the sun goes down.

We make all potential guests aware of this *before* they arrive – and it's never been an issue.

You'll have ideas about house rules you'll want to apply to your own rental too, and as long as your list doesn't become too long – or too draconian – it shouldn't be a problem, *providing* your guests are aware of what's involved.

It's unreasonable – and a bit underhand too – to accept a booking and only then reveal the rules governing a guest's stay. (Especially if it would've influenced their decision whether or not to book with you had they known about these beforehand).

Reviews – The Good and The Bad

Whatever your feelings about them, it has to be accepted that opinions expressed by your guests can have a major impact – for good and bad – on your business.

We're now long-used to seeing photos and comments from guests appearing on social media during their stay with us. It's a modern fact of life, and as I'm one for posting similar content too, I'd be a bit hypocritical if I were to take this amiss.

At the very least – it keeps you on your toes !

There are a bewildering number of sites where you can find comments about the experiences of your rental guests. Some of these will get posted without any prompting from you. Other times, you'll have to ask a guest if they'd please write a few (hopefully favourable) comments about their stay.

But because you can't realistically ask your guests to obligingly supply reviews for everywhere your rental's listed, stick with the only one that really matters – *TripAdvisor*.

Because it's a huge and globally-recognised brand, its success, influence and reputation are now self-generating. In the past, that hasn't necessarily been entirely beneficial and positive, as it's been far too easy to post fake negative reviews that can damage a business's standing.

But *TripAdvisor* and other big players in this business are learning. In addition to your guests being able to review you, many companies are now starting to offer the facility for rental owners like you and me to review our guests !

We – and I advise you too – to actively ask for *TripAdvisor* reviews from guests. We have enough evidence that they *are* read, and they *do* influence decisions about where to go on holiday.

But on the other hand, do bad reviews make potential guests *less* likely to book a stay with you ? It depends...

If you've got a healthy stack of 4- and 5-star reviews, then just a couple of 1- or 2-star feedbacks shouldn't have that much effect. People who regard checking reviews as a crucial part of the holiday choice process are usually very savvy in this area and will understand that provided pretty well all your other reviews are good, the occasional bad one just goes to show you can't please all your guests all the time.

By the law of averages, no matter how good a place is, sooner or later, somebody's not going to like it !

Of more importance than the fact you actually have a bad review, is what a guest has disliked about their stay at your rental.

Any adverse comment about the cleanliness and/or general state of repair of your property, plus the furnishings, fixtures and fittings; or – especially - any negative feedback about you/your partner personally can be seriously damaging.

With all reviews – good or bad – you have the right of reply, and – importantly – yours will be the last word on the issue.

As with the guidance above about dealing with disputes in person, responding to a bad review is similar. You're of course very sorry to hear your guest found fault – but...

- If you feel a bad review is unreasonable, don't be afraid of saying so. One of the best defences against a negative review is a large number of positive ones. If you have these – mention them. If any of these positive reviews favourably report on an aspect of your rental which is being criticised in a negative review – mention that too.

As long as you remain calm and polite, you can defend yourself as vigorously as you like.

- If you feel a guest maybe has a point, your response will be governed by what that point actually is. Remember though that whatever you write will be printed alongside your guest's comments – and will stay there for potential future guests to read.

- Because – by submitting a negative review - your guest is drawing attention to an alleged shortcoming sometime after the event, it's always a good response to express regret that your attention wasn't drawn *during their stay* to whatever was thought to be wrong, so you could have immediately done something about it, rather than find out when it was too late to do anything.

If your response starts getting heated – or over-heated ! - you might well find it's not published – so tread carefully. Sorrow is more effective than anger...

However...the fact is that no matter how hard you try, and despite your best intentions, things *can* go wrong. You *can* make mistakes. There *may* be perfectly valid reasons why on a particular occasion, an aspect of your rental genuinely hasn't been as good as it should have been.

Everyone has an occasional bad day at the office – but just be aware you can't have too many. If your negative reviews starts mounting up, you're going to run out of excuses and explanations pretty quickly – and your business is going to take a downward turn you'll find it difficult to reverse.

Looking After Your Property

No matter how respectful and careful your guests are when they're staying with you, your rentals will need upkeep, and what's inside will need periodic replacement.

As regards keeping our own rentals in good decorative order, we adopt a 'little and often' approach by touching-up any paintwork immediately it's needed, rather than wait and do a major redecoration. One great advantage of being based in Italy is that the tiled floors in our villas are *much* easier to look after than carpets !

You'll find that things can regularly just stop working, or start showing signs of wear and tear and need replacing. I'm not sure how many wall-clocks we've got through – or why ? - and the same goes for soap dishes in the shower; pots and pans; and kitchen knives ! We find it's useful to put aside a small amount from each booking into a Contingency Fund just for this purpose.

Buying good quality furniture and fittings at the outset has served us well and proved an excellent investment.

Outside, we learned very quickly that you can't micro-manage an acre of land. The area round our pool is intensively planted, but most of our outdoor space is essentially grassland – I'd never call it 'lawn' ! - that's kept in check with regular cutting.

If you've got anything more than a garden-sized plot to take care of, getting good quality cutters and mowers at the outset is a good move.

Items that are beyond our competence and experience to look after – like for example anything to do with the electrics and the plumbing for which technical qualifications are legally-required – are regularly serviced and checked by professionals. Outside, our olive trees need the care and expertise that only one of our local farmer friends can provide !

But that's about as far as it goes.

As I told you much earlier, when we started out, we bought-in a lot of outside help, but by watching and learning how the simple jobs were done, (and increasingly, some of the not-so-simple ones as well), we gradually learned to do most of the regular maintenance and upkeep tasks ourselves.

In doing this, we've appreciably decreased the amount of money we need to set aside to pay for having this work done.

It's worth underlining that if you'd told me when we started that both Pauline and I would be picking up these skills – which we didn't have the remotest idea about at the time – I'd have laughed. I'm now as amazed as anyone that we *can* do this kind of work, and if you can manage to acquire the ability to do this too, you'll gain an equal benefit.

The question we get asked more than any other is whether we've ever had any regrets about leaving the UK; moving to a different country; and launching ourselves into a business about which we knew basically nothing.

The honest answer now is – no. No regrets at all. But you might have got a different reply if you'd asked us during our first year or so here.

It was very difficult. Neither of us spoke much Italian – and in the area of rural Abruzzo we settled, nobody spoke any English at all. The period between October 2007 (when we arrived) and late March 2009 (when we moved into our new house) was spent in...er...fairly basic rental accommodation, with all our worldly good, furniture and possessions crammed into a leaky shed alongside.

The first time it flooded, we stacked everything on piles of bricks and in the end lost only the seat of one dining chair – which was eaten by mice !

Bit by bit, things got better. Our Italian improved. We began to find our way round a bit better. We met a few other Brits. Our business started. And people began booking !

No, of course it hasn't been sunshine and wine all the way, but we live in such a beautiful setting in tranquil, unspoiled countryside that it makes even the difficult times easier to get through.

And would we ever go back to the UK ? (That's the second most-asked question !) Who knows ? As much as we our lives in Italy – never say never...

Now – it's your turn...
Getting hold of this book was possibly your first step in following us into a new life and new business running a holiday rental.

And now you've worked your way through, you're maybe thinking:

- YES !

- Still not sure...

- Never in million years !

If the first answer - why not start jotting down a few ideas, and making a few preliminary outline plans ? It won't cost you anything and who knows – maybe it might whet your appetite even more and be the start of your own adventure !

If the second answer – next time you're staying in a holiday rental, talk to the owner. A lot of our guests are intrigued by what we've done and wonder whether it'd be right for them. I know of one or two who've started-up rentals businesses – but even more have either bought holiday homes in Abruzzo, or are now living here permanently.

And if wild horses would now never drag you away from where you currently are – then consider whatever you paid for this book a fair price for finding that out !

If you *do* end up going through with setting up your own rental after reading this – then I'd love to hear about it. I'm easy enough to find on Facebook – so drop me a line.

Thanks again for buying this book – and the best of luck with whatever your future plans might be.

Printed in Great Britain
by Amazon